T0193202

A Transformed
WOMAN
Will Embrace the
Transforming
GOD

A Transformed
WOMAN
Will Embrace the
Transforming
GOD

JOSEPHINE MONU

WESTBOW
PRESS®
A DIVISION OF THOMAS NELSON
& ZONDERVAN

WestBow Press books may be ordered through booksellers or by contacting:

WestBow Press
A Division of Thomas Nelson & Zondervan
1663 Liberty Drive
Bloomington, IN 47403
www.westbowpress.com
1 (866) 928-1240

Scripture taken from the King James Version of the Bible.

Scripture taken from the New King James Version. Copyright © 1979, 1980, 1982 by Thomas Nelson, Inc. Used by permission. All rights reserved.

All Scripture quotations in this publications are from The Message. Copyright © by Eugene H. Peterson 1993, 1994, 1995, 1996, 2000, 2001, 2002. Used by permission of NavPress Publishing Group.

Scripture taken from the *Amplified Bible*, copyright © 1954, 1958, 1962, 1964, 1965, 1987 by The Lockman Foundation. Used by permission.

Scripture taken from The Living Bible copyright © 1971 by Tyndale House Foundation. Used by permission of Tyndale House Publishers Inc., Carol Stream, Illinois 60188. All rights reserved. The Living Bible, TLB, and the The Living Bible logo are registered trademarks of Tyndale House Publishers.

ISBN: 978-1-5127-0880-6 (sc)
ISBN: 978-1-5127-0879-0 (hc)
ISBN: 978-1-5127-0878-3 (e)

Library of Congress Control Number: 2015913440

Print information available on the last page.

WestBow Press rev. date: 9/9/2015

To my heavenly Father, God Almighty; to my
Lord and Savior, Jesus Christ; and to the Holy
Spirit, my comforter and treasured friend

Contents

ACKNOWLEDGMENTS

I want to use this opportunity to thank my husband and our five wonderful children for all their prayers, love, support, and encouragement.

Darl, thank you for believing in me, for always encouraging me to walk in the full potential God has given me, for always reminding me of who I am in Him, and for not letting me get lazy with my God-given talents. Even when I had yet to figure out God's purpose for my life, you already knew, and you kept nudging and encouraging me to go in the right direction. I love you—always will—and I am so thankful God brought us together.

And to you, my dear, wonderful children, my cheerleaders, my wonderful blessings from God, I say a big thank you. Like your dad, you all have encouraged and supported me in your own unique ways, telling me I can do this. Ify and John, despite your very, very busy schedules, you took the time to patiently read through this book and give me your honest thoughts. I appreciate that you did this for me. I cannot thank you enough. Chika, thank you for all your prayers and prophetic words of encouragement, which were always timely. Gladys and Ngozi, thank you for always being there to make me laugh whenever I was feeling a little stressed out and wondering if I was doing the right thing. Here we are today! Praise the Lord! I could not have finished this book without all of you cheering me on. I love you all, and I am thankful to God for the privilege of being your mother.

A special thanks to my mom. Mom, you have always wanted the best for me. I love you, Mom!

To my sister, Elizabeth, I say thank you for being you. I couldn't have asked for a more wonderful sister. Love you, Sis! A special thanks also to Dr. Oluwasayo Ajiboye, who, despite his extremely busy schedule, took the time to write the foreword to this book. And to his wife, Pastor Moni, I say thank you for all your prayers and support.

FOREWORD

I write to acknowledge the great gift that God has given us in this book, *A Transformed Woman Will Embrace the Transforming God*. Most books aim to distill, refine, and deliver a higher thought, and they also seek to do it in a format that can be easily used. Few books, however, claim the eternal goal of *birthing the wisdom* that *brings transformation*. This book holds a unique distinction of seeking to birth change and impact eternity.

Transformation is about a change in status and location; it is about a movement from one state of being into another. Mrs. Josephine Monu has truly received the manna that will assist people to make this transition. As I write this foreword, I cannot take my mind off the apostolic revelation that Christ Jesus has "delivered us from the power of darkness, and hath translated us into the kingdom of his dear Son" (Col.1:13 KJV).

I also cannot shake the feeling that this book is going to be God's tool for facilitating a lot of transformations.

There are different kinds of rivers; each kind is defined by its source. Some rivers are late-stage manifestations of earlier expressions; some are middle-stage runoffs from melted snow. Few rivers, however, take their roots (yes, rivers have roots!) high up in the mountains. They spring forth like a well in God's great high places. There is no impurity in their surroundings; there are no external deposits to complicate their compositions. Such rivers spring forth and are marked only by their closeness to the ethereal reality of cloudy heavens. Such rivers are not just pure; they are the epitome of that which is sustainable; they represent what will last.

This book is like such a spring high up in the mountains. It issues forth out of cracks from which you little expect anything to flow. It started its journey far away from the noisy shouts of human crowds. Dirty feet of diseased minds have not trampled it. This river is a flow of clear waters. God sent it to soothe those who are truly thirsty; it is a gift of heaven. Such, my friends, is this book and its writer.

Please take this book, and learn from it the mysteries that it explains. Look into the life of Joseph, peep quickly into the experience of our mothers, Sarah and Mary; learn from the saints who impacted their days and are people we will look up to for eternity. Mrs. Monu has done an excellent work. In writing this book, she obviously has stayed on the mountains and has allowed the burdens of the Lord to crack her heart; from the cracks now flow this little alabaster box of beautiful ointment of words. Please take it, read it, and be transformed.

Dr. Oluwasayo Ajiboye
President
Redeemed Christian Bible College and Seminary Greenville, Texas

Introduction

God is faithful! The Bible says He will not withhold anything good from those who walk along His paths (Ps. 84:11). He always makes all grace abound toward you, so that you always have all sufficiency in all things for every good work (2 Cor. 9:8). God wants us to prosper and be in health. But if we continually resist Him and keep walking in our own ways, we can only go so far. Because He is the one who gives seed to the sower. He is the one who inspires and shows His children the way they should go. God is the one who opens doors that no one can shut, and He shuts doors no one can open. He is the way maker! And when we yield to Him, He perfects all that concerns us. In other words, He beautifies us with His glory, clothes us with His righteousness, and gives us His peace.

The day I was first inspired to begin writing on this topic—"A transformed woman will embrace the transforming God" (Jer. 31:22 MSG)—by the Lord, I did not think I could. There I was, on my knees, reading my Bible and praying the Scriptures as I read along, when all of a sudden, it was like a light switch came on, and I knew this was what the Lord wanted me to do. I was asking for a seed, and He gave me this. At first, I was a little anxious about what to write, but God—in His love and mercy—showed me the way to go. He knew what He had put on the inside of me, and He did not want me guilty of wasting His talent. It has been a journey, a wonderful one, and a journey worth taking. Studying the Scriptures and meditating on them, having the Holy Spirit inspire me day after day and show me things, has been a blessing.

My prayer is that you will be greatly blessed as you read this book. And as you allow the Holy Spirit of God to take you on a journey of transformation, may you too experience God's transforming power in your life and embrace Him. I can tell you my life experienced changes as I worked on this book. God bless you as you take this journey with me!

Chapter 1

THE TRANSFORMING GOD

In the beginning was the Word and the Word was with God,
and the Word was God ... All things were made by him; and
without him was not anything made that was made.

—JOHN 1:1, 3 (KJV)

In the beginning, God spoke the entire world into existence. There is nothing in existence today that God did not command. The Bible tells us that He speaks and makes good on His Word. He is not a man that He should lie (Num. 23:19). His Word is true, and He is true to His Word. His Word is so powerful that He, God, magnified His Word above His own name (Ps. 138:2). Isn't that awesome? The Bible says that Scripture, God's written Word, His promise to us, cannot be broken. It is written, "Till heaven and earth pass away, one jot or one tittle will by no means pass from the law" (Matt. 5:18, NKJV). God is the Alpha and the Omega, the beginning and the end! He is the all-sufficient God, the one who is God all by Himself, who is the Creator of the ends of the earth.

Because of the magnitude of His greatness, words cannot fully describe God. He is so holy, so just, and righteous all together. God says of Himself in Isaiah 46:9–10 (KJV), "For I am God, and there is none else; I am God, and there is none like me, declaring the end from the beginning, and from ancient times the things that are not yet done, saying My counsel shall stand, and I will do all my pleasure." Because of who He is and because of His awesome power, God is able to exceed all that we can ask or think. Where love is lacking, He supplies love; where forgiveness is needed, He gives it; where compassion is needed, He extends it; where there is guilt, shame, and reproach, He removes and covers it with His love, grace, and forgiveness. Wherever there is a need, He meets that need. He is a wonderful shepherd and a great provider! He is the one who gives power to get wealth (Deut. 8:18). He is God. He is God all by Himself! He goes before us and makes ways where there have been no ways; He restores the soul of the backslider in heart; He leads in paths of righteousness for His name's sake (Ps. 23:3). And He is always with us—Immanuel, God with us! He never leaves us or forsakes us (Deut. 31:6). He is the very present help in the time of trouble or need (Ps.46:1;Isa.41:10). He is in us (John 17:23), our hope of glory (Rom. 5:2). Amen.

In Isaiah 44:6–7 (KJV), it is written of the Lord, the King of Israel, "I am the first, and I am the last; and beside me there is no God. And who, as I, shall call, and shall declare it, and set it in order for me, since I appointed the ancient people?" God calls those things that do not exist as though they did (Rom. 4:17). He says, "Let there be," and things happen; they come into existence (Gen. 1). He makes things happen for you and for me because He is able, because He is all sufficient, and because He has the power, for all power in heaven and earth belongs to Him.

God has the ability to transform the life of an individual, to change circumstances for His glory, and to make all things new again in anyone's life. He is the one who can transform a sinner into a saint. He is the one true God! Honestly, I do not think that there is anyone on earth, no matter how hard he or she tried, who could even begin to describe Him. To God alone belongs all power in heaven and earth. God alone has the power to transform the life of an individual, to make great, to give strength to all, to give wealth, and to turn any bad situation around.

Chapter 2

IN THE IMAGE OF GOD

And God said, Let us make man in our image, after our
likeness ... So God created man in his own image, in the image
of God created he him; male and female created he them.
—GENESIS 1:26–27 (KJV)

The heart of God the Father has always been that we are like Him. This is why He created man (us) in His own image, after His likeness. The fall of man in the garden of Eden (see Gen. 3) changed things, however. Man ceased to be and live as God desired. Sin not only came into the world, but it also became part of man's nature. David exclaims in Psalm 51:5, "But I was born a sinner, yes, from the moment my mother conceived me" (LB). Sin separated man from fellowship with God; it became a powerful force in the lives of men, but God never stopped loving man and wanting him back—to be like Him again. God initiated a plan to bring us back to Him, to become like Him—through Jesus's death on the cross—and He has never stopped working in our hearts since then, just so we can help fulfill His plan on earth. After all, we were created for His pleasure and purpose!

Throughout the Scriptures, we see stories of men and women whose lives were transformed by God. We see a clear example of a life that was dramatically transformed by the power of the Most High in the life of a man called Saul, who was once a sinner and who later became known as Paul the apostle. Before Saul converted, he wreaked havoc on the church, entering into every house and hauling men and women to prison (Acts 8:3), until the day the Lord met him on his way to Damascus. Suddenly, everything changed for Saul from that day on. Even his name changed (Acts 9:1–26; 13:9). Paul's life transformation can be summed up in this one sentence, as he put it in Galatians 2:20 (KJV): "Yet not I, but Christ liveth in me: and the life which I now live in the flesh I live by the faith of the Son of God, who loved me, and gave himself for me." Paul's life had been so transformed that he saw his life through God's eyes.

Then we have this man called Joseph. Here was a young man, talented but full of himself. He lacked wisdom, and he told on his brothers and was a little prideful because of his father's love for him (Gen. 37:2–3). Because of this, his brothers really hated him, and they envied him too.

Now, through a series of circumstances, Joseph became a transformed man. Even his language changed. He no longer spoke proudly or foolishly, but he spoke with the fear of the Lord in him. In Genesis 39:9 (KJV), Joseph said to Potiphar's wife, "How then can I do this great wickedness, and sin against God?" Despite repeated pressures from Potiphar's wife, Joseph feared God enough to resist the pressure of temptation coming his way. He had become a God-fearing man who walked in kindness and forgiveness.

God so worked in Joseph's life that he gave glory to God for every opportunity he had after he got out of prison. His language became one of acknowledging God's sovereignty, God's power, and God's might. His language was also one of worship and reverence for God. He never once tried to share in God's glory; he was very careful to give God all the glory. When he talked to people, he tried to point them to God. When he was talking to Pharaoh about his dream,

> "Joseph said unto Pharaoh … God hath shewed Pharaoh what he is about to do … This is the thing which I have spoken unto Pharaoh: What God is about to do he sheweth unto Pharaoh … And for that the dream was doubled … it is because the thing is established by God, and God will shortly bring it to pass" (Gen. 41:25, 28, 32, KJV).

Even when Joseph was talking with his brothers, he was careful to point his brothers to God. He did not dare take the glory for himself:

> "Now therefore be not grieved … for God did send me before you to preserve life … And God sent me before you to preserve you posterity in the earth, and to save your lives by a great deliverance. So now it was not you that sent me hither, but God: and he hath made me a father to Pharaoh" (Gen. 45:5, 7–8, KJV).

The transformation in Joseph's life did not stop with his language. His entire character had changed. He was now a very humble man, one who no longer saw himself as the one being bowed down to. His suggestion to Pharaoh to appoint "a man discreet and wise" to oversee the land in preparation for the coming years of famine (Gen. 41:33, KJV) tells us that the old Joseph no longer lived. Joseph did not think himself wise and discreet, but Pharaoh saw him as that: "And Pharaoh said unto Joseph, Forasmuch as God hath shewed thee all this, there is none so discreet and wise as thou art" (Gen. 41:39). This new, transformed Joseph, who was now changed by the transforming God, was a caring man. He showed concern for his father and his younger brother, Benjamin, whom he had not seen in a long time. He cared that his brothers who sold him into slavery had enough food for their families. When God's power is at work, people's lives are changed dramatically.

Still, taking a closer look at Joseph, we see that even his attitude toward the things of God changed. He became a man who feared God. In Genesis 48:12–19, we see Joseph's willingness to respect God's covenant about firstborns. After the death of his father, we see a man unwilling to take revenge on his brothers for what they did to him; he was a man who recognized that it was not his place to act as God and judge them for their wickedness (Gen. 50:19). Instead, he tried to help them understand God's plan (Gen. 50:20). We see a transformed Joseph, a man who has become forgiving, understanding, humble, kind, and gentle.

Before Joseph was his father, Jacob, who was transformed from being a "deceiver" (Gen. 27:12) to a man who feared God, honored God and His covenant, and became known as Israel, "a prince of God" (Gen. 32:28). Then you have Moses, one who stammered, with no confidence in himself, a fearful, insecure man who confronted Pharaoh and who became a friend of God (Ex. 33:11). And the list goes on (see Hebrews 11). This is what the transforming power of the almighty, transforming God at work in our lives can do in us, with us, for us and through us. Amen!

God is daily and constantly working in us and transforming us for His purpose and for His glory. He does this through His Holy Spirit working in us. It is written, "For it is God which worketh in you both to will and to do of his good pleasure" (Phil. 2:13 KJV). The power to transform is God's and God's alone. His transforming, creative power is so awesome that the worldly wise are usually confounded by it (1 Cor. 1:27).

Chapter 3

TRANSFORMED

But be transformed (changed) *by the [entire] renewal
of your mind [by its new ideals and its new attitude], so
that you may prove [for yourselves] what is the good and
acceptable and perfect will of God, even the thing which is
good and acceptable and perfect [in his sight for you].*
—ROMANS 12:2 (AB EMPHASIS ADDED)

What does the word *transformed* really mean? And how does a
person become transformed? Simply put, the word *transformed*
means "changed." According to the *New Strong's Expanded Dictionary
of Bible Words*, this word in the Greek means "to undergo a complete
change which under the power of God will find expression in character
and conduct."

Second Corinthians 3:18 tells us, "But we all, with open face
beholding as in a glass the glory of the Lord, are changed into the same
image from glory to glory, even as by the Spirit of the Lord" (KJV).
In other words, a God encounter usually brings about changes such

as these. For the more we yield to the Spirit of the Lord, the more the Lord works in our lives: "For it is God who works in you both to will and to do for His good pleasure" (Phil. 2:13 NKJV).

The Bible is full of stories of people whose lives were changed by the power of God. Some changes were instantaneous, and some came through a process of time. But all worked for good for the individuals to the glory of God. Transformation begins immediately at the very moment an individual invites Jesus into his or her heart and asks Him to be his or her Lord and Savior. But I dare say that the process never stops. It is ongoing! God never stops working in us. His purpose and desire for us is for Christ to be truly formed in us so that we can have a future and a hope (Jer. 29:11). So as this change begins to occur on the inside of that individual (within the heart, that is), God sees, and God knows. "For the Lord does not see as man sees; for man looks at the outward appearance, but the Lord looks at the heart" (1 Sam. 16:7).

The Self-Righteous Group

"There is a class of people who are pure in their own eyes, and yet are not washed from their own filth" (Prov. 30:12 AB).

"Because you say, 'I am rich, have become wealthy, and have need of nothing'—and do not know that you are wretched, miserable, poor, blind, and naked" (Rev. 3:17 NKJV).

"As it is written, None is righteous, just and truthful and upright and conscientious, no, not one ... All have turned aside; together they have gone wrong and have become unprofitable and worthless; no one does right, not even one!" (Rom. 3:10, 12 AB).

Some people may say, "I have never asked Jesus to be my Lord and Savior, but I have always been good," or "I have never done anything bad or hurtful to anyone in my life," or "I have never smoked a day in my life," or "I have never cheated on my spouse; I have always been faithful." We could go on with a long list of good things. All may be true, but the real question here is this: how does God see you and all of your so-called "good works"? You see, as 1 Samuel 16:7 says, God looks at the heart and not our attempts at trying to appear good or to impress.

The Bible tells of the story of a rich young ruler who came to Jesus with his works. Remember him? (If you don't, you can read his story in Luke 18:18–23.) This young ruler came to Christ to ask what he had to do "to inherit eternal life." He was rich, young, and feeling good about himself. He, trusting in his own righteousness, asked an honest yet simple question about eternal life. He called Jesus "Good Master" (indicating reverence or a show of respect—a good thing that is lacking in today's world). To the casual observer, this was a respectful, religious man who wanted to know more about the faith in which he believed. Judging from his response to Jesus's reply about keeping the Ten Commandments ("all these have I kept from my youth up" Luke 18:21 KJV), one would have to agree that he was a sure candidate for heaven. Both his question and his response present a picture-perfect Christian to the world. Underneath the entire façade, however, was a questionable character with a truly selfish heart. Jesus knew he still lacked sincerity in his life, and so he threw a challenge at him, just to test him: "Sell all that thou hast … and come, follow me" (Luke 18:22). Guess what? He failed the test. How? He walked away sad; he did not want to do what Jesus asked him to do. The true state of his heart was exposed—that he was a selfish and pretentious man. It was and had always been about him, his own self-righteousness, his will, and his accomplishments and not God's. This man actually believed his righteousness and his deeds qualified him. Nevertheless, when examined under God's all-seeing eyes, he failed. The Bible says he went away feeling "distressed and very sorrowful" (Luke 18:23 AB). Jesus was not demanding that he sell his entire wealth. He was helping this ruler see that his motives were not what he presented to the world. He wanted him to reexamine his heart and to see that he still lacked something vital and very important to his salvation—a willingness to surrender all to the One who gave it all. Jeremiah 17:9 says "the heart is deceitful above all things, and desperately wicked: who can know it?" (KJV). Who can know what is in the thought and intents of the heart except the Lord? Any other person hearing the words of this ruler might say that he was truly a godly man, a true believer. When standing before the One who sees all things and knows all things, however, the one and only true God, nothing is hidden. He is a revealer of secrets. God's Word discerns the thoughts and intents of our hearts, and Jesus, the living word of God, discerned and exposed the thoughts and intents of this man's heart. No one is good except God only.

So let us allow God's Word to examine our hearts before we declare ourselves to be good. It is a proud heart that sees things his way and his way alone—"Woe unto them that are wise in their own eyes, and prudent in their own sight!" (Isa. 5:21 KJV)—but a humble heart not only has that holy, reverential fear of God but also sees things the way God would have him see because he has the mind of Christ. Pride has no place in the presence of the Almighty.

The Self-Proclaimed Changed Group

> "There is a class of people—oh, how lofty are their eyes
> and their raised eyelids!" (Prov. 30:13 AB).

"All have strayed away; all are rotten with sin.
Not one is good, not one!" (Ps. 14:3 LB).

"For all have sinned and fall short of the
glory of God" (Rom. 3:23 NKJV).

In addition to the self-righteous group is a group of people who may argue, "I certainly did not ask Jesus into my heart to be my Lord and Savior, but I do know that I am a changed person," or "I used to do a lot of drugs, but I don't do drugs anymore," or "I used to be an alcoholic, but I don't drink anymore. I am a changed man [or woman]." All of this may be true, but true change never begins if it does not originate in Jesus Christ. The Bible says we are complete in Jesus Christ and "in Him dwells the fullness of the Godhead" (Col. 2:9 NKJV). Jesus said, "I am the way, the truth, and the life. No one comes to the Father except through Me" (John 14:6 NKJV). All a person does by living life without Christ is set himself up for setbacks. What he is doing is like building a house on sand (the confidence he puts in his own ability and strength), and when the storms of life (trials and temptations) come, it washes away the weak foundation. And what happens thereafter? The person's whole world comes crumbling down (see Matthew 7:24–29). Like Jesus said to the rich young ruler, "There is still one thing you lack" (Luke 18:22 LB), and that is salvation. I believe Jesus may be saying the same thing to you today, that you still lack His saving power. For the power to save and to bring about a change in your life is not in you but in Him and Him alone.

In Isaiah 64:5–6, it is written, "But we are not godly; we are constant sinners and have been all our lives … How can such as we be saved? We are all infected and impure with sin. When we put on our prized robes of righteousness, we find they are but filthy rags" (LB).

The King James Version puts it this way: "But we are all as an unclean thing, and *all our righteousnesses are as filthy rags*" (emphasis added). So how then can we think that our own righteousness will make ways for us when Jesus is the way and the only way? "For He made Him who knew no sin to be sin for us, that we might become the righteousness of God in Him" (2 Cor. 5:21 NKJV). Would you let Jesus in? You do not have to work on you all by yourself. Jesus wants to give you rest. He will give you the grace you need. Let Him in, and He will make all things new and beautiful for you (Eccl. 3:11). So let the change begin in you right now. Ask Jesus to come into your heart and be your Lord and Savior. Repent of all your sinful ways, and let Him take the lead.

Transformation through the Holy Spirit

Now, as the Holy Spirit of God daily convicts us of sin, righteousness, and of judgment, the process of transformation continues, and we find ourselves changing from glory to glory. As we continue to willingly yield to the promptings of the Holy Spirit, our hearts increasingly long for more of God and more of His heartbeat. We want what He wants, and like Paul, we begin to count all things as dung (Phil. 3:8), and our language becomes, "I myself no longer live, but Christ lives in me. And the real life I now have within this body is a result of my trusting in the Son of God, who loved me and gave himself for me" (Gal. 2:20 LB).

Unholy and unrighteous ways give way to Jesus, the Way. We die daily, and like Paul, we are confident about the change going on in us. We boldly say, "I die daily" (1 Cor. 15:31 KJV). This, dear friend, is transformation through the power of God. As believers, we should die daily to self, just as change for good and for God's glory should be a daily occurrence in our lives. This is the beauty of living in Christ!

Colossians 3:3 says, "For [as far as this world is concerned] you have died, and your [new, real] life is hidden with Christ in God" (AB). The more we yield to God, the more change He brings in our characters. We just have to be willing and obedient to His Word and also sensitive to His Holy Spirit, so that when He, the Spirit of truth, comes wanting to effect yet another change in us, we graciously and reverentially will surrender to His touch, so that we can go from glory to glory.

I often pray along these lines: *Dear Lord, dig deeper into my heart, and anything you see that is not pleasing to you root out, so that I can become who you have called me to be.* And guess what? The Holy Spirit comes and pinpoints those things that need to be laid down, things that I need to repent of or turn away from that do not glorify God. Almost immediately, I begin to see things not from my own perspective but from the Lord's. In the book of Psalms, David says, "Search me, O God … Point out anything you find in me that makes you sad, and lead me along the path of everlasting life" (139:23–24 LB). Isn't this a beautiful prayer request? May the longing of your soul be to please your heavenly Father all the days of your life; may your heart cry, "More of you, Lord, in my life!" Praise God! God is so willing to work in you, to beautify you with His glory. But the big question here is this: are you willing to let Him into your life to do what only He can do for you? To bring the transformation that He only can perfect in your life? Because, you see, it is not all about you but about Him and His kingdom, and knowing this truth makes it easier to yield to His Holy Spirit.

Chapter 4

THE MAKING OF
ANOTHER VESSEL

And the vessel that he was making ... was spoiled in the hand
of the potter; so he made it over, reworking it into another
vessel as it seemed good to the potter to make it.

—Jeremiah 18:4 (AB)

Now let us look at some women in the Bible who had divine experiential encounters. Their encounters with God caused them to go through the precious process of transformation. I say "precious" because money cannot buy this work of the Holy Spirit in a person's life. No wonder David exclaimed in Psalm 139:17, "How precious also are thy thoughts unto me, O God! How great is the sum of them!" (KJV). God's thoughts toward you are to do you good, not evil; to bring you to that place of glory and honor (Jer. 29:11). The process each and every one of these women underwent caused their mind to be renewed. Submission of their lives and will to God's purposes for them—a walk in truth, humility, and the fear of God—caused them to become women of great character, great faith, and love.

Our first example is Mary, the mother of Jesus. But before we take a closer look at her, you must understand that a divine encounter with God (e.g., salvation experience, giving your life to Jesus) must first take place before transformation takes place. Then and only then can a person experience the kind of change or transformation talked about in this book.

Mary, the mother of Jesus: Mary was a young and perhaps a very shy lady. The Bible describes her as a "virgin" (Luke 1:27 KJV). She was to be married to Joseph, of the lineage of David. A day came when she had a divine visitation that changed her entire life forever. The Bible tells us that the angel Gabriel was sent from God to Mary with news that boggled her mind (Luke 1:26–35). This quiet, gentle soul, not popular or famous in any way, who had to endure shame and embarrassment for the duration of her pregnancy, even before she was married, through no fault of her own after a divine encounter (Matt. 1:18), suddenly became a woman of honor (Luke 1:28).

Let us look at the journey that took her to this place of honor. Mary was a young woman, a virgin, who found herself pregnant. One can only imagine how challenging that time was for the young girl. Yet Mary chose to believe God. She looked to Him because she had come to know Him. As a result of the divine encounter with the angel of the Lord, she had learned in an instant what it meant to submit to the will of God (Luke 1:38). You know, when you learn to submit your will to the Lord's, life becomes easier because God will fight for you. Because Mary submitted totally to God, taking Him at His word, God arose on her behalf (Matt. 1:19–25). I believe that during Mary's pregnancy, she had to renew her mind, meditating on God's Word (His precious promise to her through His angel) on a daily basis, until she came to totally trust in the Lord with all her heart, not leaning on her own understanding (Prov. 3:5). Friend, there is hope for you. Meditate on God's Word daily! Let it refresh you, and let it renew your mind. The book of James says, "Let patience have her perfect work, that ye may be perfect and entire, wanting nothing" (1:4). God can take a broken vessel and mend it. He can repair whatever has been damaged in your life, no matter how bad the damage is. He can make you whole again. Another thing we must remember about Mary is that having watched her son Jesus grow and having seen God working through Him, she got to know more about God's faithfulness. The psalmist says, "O taste and see that the Lord is good" (Ps. 34:8 KJV).

Well, Mary did, and having tasted of the Lord's goodness, she did not want it any other way. Because of Jesus and because of the work of transformation that had taken place in her life, Mary refused to depart from following the Lord. She was there when Jesus went to the cross. She did not depart from following Him, even after His death. She remained faithful! She was even among the disciples waiting for the baptism of the Holy Spirit in the upper room: "These all continued with one accord in prayer and supplication, with the women, *and Mary the mother of Jesus* and with his brethren" (Acts 1:13–14 KJV, emphasis added). During the early ministry of Jesus, we see the old Mary try to interrupt Jesus while He was ministering to the people. She stood outside, instead of inside with the people (Matt 12:46–50). But the new, transformed Mary stood by Jesus when He was on the cross (John 19:25–26). This "new creation" in Christ Jesus was not ashamed of the gospel of Jesus Christ, nor was she afraid to identify with Christ (remember, she was there at His crucifixion). She could have gone into hiding or denied Jesus, but no! She remained in Him; she remained close to Him. Praise the Lord!

The woman at the well: Maybe your life story is almost like the woman at the well, the Samaritan woman (John 4:7–29). Perhaps, like her, you have had more than one husband, have lived an adulterous life, and are full of guilt and shame and have nowhere to turn or no one to turn to. Well, I have good news for you. The Bible tells us that "there is a friend who sticks closer than a brother" (Prov. 18:24 NKJV). His name is Jesus; His name is Counselor. He is the Prince of Peace, and He can give you the rest you need (Isa. 9). Turn to Him even now and say, "Dear Lord Jesus, come into my heart. Come and be my Lord and Savior. Rescue me from death, and give me your life that I may have eternal life. And please write my name in the Lamb's Book of Life. In Your precious name I pray. Amen!" This simple prayer makes a whole world of difference in a person's life.

The woman of Samaria dared herself to ask ("Sir, give me this water, that I not thirst" [John 4:15 KJV]), and she did receive the love of Christ. She wanted more than anything the life that Christ was offering her, and her life was changed for her good forever. Hear her testimony. "Come see a man who knew all about the things I did, who knows me inside and out" (John 4:29 MSG). This woman's story—or should I say her testimony—drew others out of their doubts and comfort zones to go seek the one true Messiah, to see who it was who had caused such a dramatic change in the life of a woman they all knew so well. To them, this woman was a woman with a very bad history. She was no stranger at all to anyone in the city, and having a history like she did (having five husbands and living in sin at that time), they just had to come see the cause of the change in her life for themselves. She probably had a sudden glow around her, a brilliance they could not explain, joy inexpressible and full of glory.

You know, an encounter with the Lord will cause a person to be radically changed, full of power, and full of His glory. Many years ago, the desire for me to be born again came as a result of my seeing this wonderful glow, brilliance, and joy inexpressible on the face of a dear friend and relative who, had, only a couple of weeks earlier, given her life to Jesus Christ. As we sat together by the dining table in the home of a family member, she began to share her story—how she was born again and all the wonderful things happening in her life. And as she talked, I could not help but notice the change in the appearance of her face. What a glow! The joy coming out of her was almost palpable. It was amazing! I could not stop thinking about her exuberant joy and the light of God's countenance radiating on her face (see Num. 6:25).

On the way home, I remember asking my husband if he had seen the glow on her face. This got me thinking about my life and about Jesus. And after that night of discussion with this dear friend and relative, I prayed daily for a while, asking the Lord what it meant to be born again and how I would know when I was born again. Then, one beautiful evening in October at a conference on the Holy Spirit in the Episcopalian church I attended, Jesus, the Way, showed up in that meeting and showed me the way to Him. I gave my life to Jesus, and I can tell you that my life has not been the same since that day. By His grace, I have never looked back or regretted my decision to follow Him.

You know, after an encounter with the living God, a person's life is never the same; transformation begins to take place on the inside right away. We see an example of this in the Bible with the men of the city of Samaria. The Bible tells us that these men believed because of the woman's report: "He told me everything that I ever did!' (John 4:39 LB). They did not just believe; they asked Jesus to stay on at their village, thus inviting Jesus into their lives (John 4:40–41). What a ripple effect of an encounter with the Lord! Hear their own report after their encounter with the divine presence. "Then they said to the woman, 'Now we believe because we have heard him ourselves, not just because of what you told us. He is indeed the Savior of the world'" (John 4:42 LB). Wow! What a declaration of faith and truth!

Who do you believe in? What is your testimony or praise report? We have to know, without a shadow of doubt, who we say we believe in. As Elijah said, "How long are you going to waver between two opinions? If the Lord is God, follow him!" (1 Kings 18:21 LB). There is no room for wavering. And I submit to you that the Lord is God, and He is the One who made us. We did not make Him, neither did we make ourselves. Psalm 100:3 says, "Know this: *God is God, and God, God.* He made us; we didn't make Him. We are His people, His well-tended sheep" (MSG, emphasis added). *The Living Bible* puts it this way: "*Try to realize what this means*—the Lord is God! He made us—we are His people, the sheep of His pasture" (emphasis mine).

Anna: Now let us take a look at another woman, one called Anna (see Luke 2:36–38). Who was she, and what made her love the house and presence of the Lord so much that for eighty-four years she did not depart from the temple, day or night (Luke 2:37)? The Bible tells us that this woman, with a wonderful background, a rich heritage (of the tribe of Asher, blessed by Jacob in Genesis 49:20), had suffered a great loss earlier in life. Her husband of just seven years died, leaving her alone, presumably without children. We can only guess that she was very young when she married, because she had been a widow for eighty-four years (Luke 2:37). Imagine that! Despite this tragedy, she experienced a transformation in her life.

From a life of tragedy, a life filled with sorrow and pain, Anna pressed into a life of joy and living life to the fullest in His presence through faith. How did she do this? She made a deliberate choice to do something and that was to worship the Lord in the beauty of His holiness. And worship Him, she did—not just worshiping Him but worshiping Him with fasting and prayers, night and day, for eighty-four good years. What a way to go! She chose to remain in God's presence, rather than walk away from His love because of her loss. She turned her hurt and loss over to the Lord and stayed there in His house. "She never left the Temple area, worshiping night and day with her fastings and prayers" (Luke 2:37 MSG). Now, if Moses, after forty days and forty nights on the mountain in God's presence, could appear before God's people with such great radiance on his face (it shone so brightly that a cloth had to be put over his face [Ex. 34]), what do you think a lifetime of uninterrupted pure worship, coupled with fasting and prayers, would do to one in His presence continually?

Transformation will take place both on the inside and on the outside of the individual involved, with patience being one of the virtues wrought by the power and glory of God in that individual. And I dare say that Anna, while worshiping God on a daily basis, learned to depend on and trust God through faith and patience (letting "patience have her perfect work" [James 1:4]), with fasting and prayers.

Now remember, Anna had every reason to be bitter and angry with God. She had no children and had plenty of time on her hands to just grieve and grieve. But she chose to remain in the courts of the Lord. Joshua said to the people of God, "Choose you this day whom ye will serve … but as for me and my house, we will serve the Lord" (Josh. 24:15 KJV). Moses said to the children of Israel in Exodus 32:26, "Who is on the Lord's side? Let him come unto me" (KJV).

I ask you today: what are the choices you have made or are about to make? Have you made a choice to be on the Lord's side? Or are you going to let bitterness, anger, resentment, and frustration make you turn away from the Lord? There is no situation that we are faced with today of which the Lord is not aware. When we hurt, He hurts also. This is why He says in His Word that all who labor and are heavy laden (working hard beneath a heavy yoke) should come to Him, and He will give them rest (Matt. 11:28). God does not want us going around carrying weights. He wants us enjoying the abundant life that He not only has promised us but also has given to us (John 10:10). Anna's life of dedication is the direct result of the inner workings of the power of God. This power transformed a young, grieving widow to one telling the good news of the merciful kindness, plan, and purpose of the living God with a joyful heart. "She … began thanking God and telling everyone in Jerusalem who had been awaiting the coming of the Savior that the Messiah had finally arrived" (Luke 2:38 LB).

Had Anna walked away from God after her tragedy, she probably would never have been privileged to be in the temple when the baby Jesus was brought in to be dedicated, and she would not have had the privilege of seeing Him or experienced the joy of telling others the good news of Jesus's arrival. Making the right choice helped put her in the position to be favored. What about you? What is your situation like?

I encourage you not to walk away from the Lord. There is hope for you and for all who are willing to let God work in them by the power of His Holy Spirit. Jesus sees you where you are, and He wants to transform your life (and your situation), if only you will let Him. He wants to give you that abundant life that He came to give us all. 1 Peter 5:10 says, "After you have suffered a little while, our God, who is full of kindness through Christ, will give you His eternal glory. He personally will come and pick you up, and set you firmly in place, and make you stronger than ever" (LB). *The Message* says, "It won't be long before this generous God who has great plans for us in Christ—eternal and glorious plans they are!—will have you put together and on your feet for good." 1 Peter 5:11 says, "He [God] gets the last word; yes, he does." Isn't that great that God has the last word concerning us and not the Devil? What a glorious thought!

Ruth: In the days before Ruth's transformation, she was referred to as "Ruth the Moabitess" (Ruth 1:22–4:10). When the days of her transformation were ended, she became known simply as "Ruth" (Ruth 4:13). Up until before this time, all that people ever thought of her was where she came from—the girl from Moab, the girl from a tribe of people God had excluded from Israel ("No Ammonite or Moabite is to enter the congregation of God, even to the tenth generation ... Don't even try to get along with them or do anything for them" [Deut. 23:3–6 MSG])—and not who she was being transformed into, a girl graced with the spirit of servanthood; a girl who willingly gave up all she ever knew to become part of God's prized family; a girl who chose to walk in obedience rather than disobedience; a girl who chose intimacy with God, forsaking her father, her mother, and the land of her nativity. It was not until they all saw the full manifestation of God's handiwork in her life (when Boaz offered to marry her, and the Lord gave her a son) that she then gained the full respect of all.

Now let us take a closer look at the story of Ruth's life to know how she came to the place of walking fully into her destiny. Once upon a time, in the days when judges led Israel, a man from Bethlehem in Judah left his home to live in the country of Moab. While there, he died, and his wife and two sons were left. Both sons married Moabite women, and the name of the first woman was Orpah, and the name of the second was Ruth. As a Moabite woman, Ruth lacked nothing, really. Though she was married to a foreigner, she still lived among her own people, and her people were wealthy and self-satisfied (see Jeremiah 48). Ruth pretty much had everything going for her.

Then a day came when everything changed for her. Her husband of about ten years died, throwing her into sorrow. Her mother-in-law, whom she may have been living with after her husband's death, decided she wanted to leave the land of Moab and return to her own land and her own people. Ruth's world of security, comfort, love, stability, wealth, self-satisfaction, and pride as she had known it was falling apart, right before her eyes. What was she to do?

Ruth decided to step out in faith by following her mother-in-law back to her land, the land of Bethlehem, to a people she never knew and who she was not sure would welcome her. But read her words to Naomi: "Your people shall be my people, and your God, my God" (Ruth 1:15 NKJV). Sometimes for us to enter into our destiny, we have to give up all we know as security and support, step out in faith, and totally depend on God for everything. Ruth was able, through faith and patience, to inherit God's promise for her life. Her declaration of faith in a God she was yet to understand fully plunged her into the blessings of God—but not in the way she may have expected it to come. The Lord took her down the road leading to humility. Remember she came out from a people who were wealthy, and so she could have had servants waiting on her and doing things for her, had she stayed in her own land. But here she was in a strange land, working as a farmhand and toiling tirelessly without pay (Ruth 2:8).

When you invite Jesus Christ into your heart to be your Lord and Savior, He sure does come and immediately leads you down His destined path for you. The psalmist said, "He leads me in the paths of righteousness for His name's sake" (Ps. 23 NKJV). Ruth asked God to be her God, and He immediately began to lead her down His path, the path of righteousness for His own name's sake. God says in Isaiah 42:16, "But I'll take the hand of those who don't know the way, who can't see where they're going. I'll be a personal guide to them, *directing them through unknown country*" (MSG, emphasis added). The King James Version puts it this way: "And I will bring the blind by a way that they knew not; I will lead them in paths that they have not known:

I will make darkness light before them, and crooked things straight. These things will I do unto them, and not forsake them."

Ruth's confession brought her into a divine encounter with the living God, and this encounter opened doors of divine favor for her before men but not without first taking her through paths unknown to her (humility, patience, and servanthood). This is what a God encounter usually does. It usually makes ways and opens doors where there had been no way or door opened before. Because Ruth allowed God to be God in her life, she was blessed beyond measure; her path ended up with her marrying into true riches—she married Boaz, a truly wealthy man of his time, and then, the truest riches of all, being the mother of a son who was in the lineage of Christ (see Ruth 4:18–22; Matthew 1:1–17).

Obedience brings the blessings! Besides walking in humility (for the fear of the Lord brings the grace to walk in humility [Prov. 22:4]), Ruth faithfully obeyed instructions from her mother-in-law (Ruth 3:3–6), thereby letting patience have its perfect work in her (James 1:4). For most of the book of Ruth (2:1–4:17), we see Ruth's language laced with politeness, courtesy, honor, respect, and humility. We see an example of this in Ruth 2:13, where she refers to herself as "your handmaiden." Although Ruth was from Moab, a place the Scriptures describes as arrogant and prideful (Jer. 48:29 KJV), she was different. Ruth had become confident in who she was in the Lord and with her mother-in-law. Her lifestyle, in general, showed that she was now really transformed, a far cry from the description of the Moabites in Jeremiah 48:29. Hear Boaz in Ruth 3:11: "For all the city of my people doth know that thou art a virtuous woman" (KJV). She was totally transformed by the power of God Most High, the one "under whose wings" she had come to trust (2:12 KJV).

Ruth had come from a place and a people who were not favored in the sight of God to a place of glory and honor, to become a people of God; she surrendered her pain from the loss of her husband, her father, and her mother and the land of her nativity for an encounter with God (Ruth 2:11). And transform her, He did, to a lifestyle of praise (3:11; 4:15) and a wonderful heritage—the lineage in Christ. So dearly beloved of God, do not let sorrow or pain stop you from wholeheartedly following or giving up your all for a lifetime of fellowship and intimacy with Him. For God Almighty knows our very end from our beginning; He knows our frame. He is God all by Himself!

The latter part of Ruth's life was better than her former because of God's transforming power working in her life. She became selfless in her service; it was no longer all about her, because she had come to learn how giving was so much better than receiving, how serving was so much more of a blessing than being served, and how obedience and humility were the key to success in life. We can conclude of Ruth that she esteemed the reproach (the role of a farmhand, which was the equivalent of being a servant) of Christ as greater riches than the treasures of Moab. By faith she endured as seeing Him who is invisible (Heb. 11:26–27). This is what God's transforming power will do in a person—to anyone who is hungry for His touch and willingly welcomes Him into his or her life. Such a one truly becomes a new creation in Christ, Old things pass away, and everything becomes new (2 Cor. 5:17). God can and is willing to make all things new for us. Praise the Lord!

Hannah: Hannah, in the book of 1 Samuel, is another woman who had the privilege of being transformed by God's divine power. She was the first wife of Elkanah: "[Elkanah] had two wives. The first was Hannah; the second was Peninnah" (1 Sam. 1:2 MSG). We are told that Peninnah had children, but Hannah did not. Could it be that her husband married another woman because she was unable to have children? If this was the situation, Hannah's emotional state of mind can only be imagined. The pain, the shame, and the humiliation of being mocked by her rival turned her into a woman full of sorrow (1 Sam. 1:6–8). Joy had gone out the window for her, though she was a woman who was greatly loved by her husband. Depression took the place of her peace, and nothing her husband did to make her happy worked. He even gave her double portions whenever they went up to Shiloh to offer the yearly sacrifice to God (1 Sam. 1:5, 8).

But none of that encouraged her or gave her peace or joy. What made this woman so depressed, so unsatisfied with life, so emotionally distraught? Barrenness! Yes, Hannah was barren, not through her own making but because "the Lord had shut up her womb" (1 Sam. 1:6 KJV). What do you do when God says no to something you want so badly? You just trust in His mercy, and like the patriarchs of old, you try to inherit His promise for you through faith and patience.

We see Hannah in her situation, having to endure all day and all night the humiliation and the shame and the reproach that came with being barren in the hands of her rival, Peninnah. Oh yes! Peninnah taunted Hannah like no man's business. She kept "rubbing it in and never letting her forget that God had not given her children" (1 Sam. 1:7 MSG). She made it her mission to scoff and laugh at Hannah, making her cry so much. The King James Version says, "And her adversary also provoked her sore, for to make her fret." Hannah cried all the time and did not eat, not because she was fasting but because her soul was crushed; "she was in bitterness of soul" (1 Sam. 1:10 KJV). Hannah describes herself as "a woman of a sorrowful spirit" (1 Sam. 1:15 KJV).

As if the taunting of her adversary, Peninnah, was not enough to make her miserable and humiliate her, in the house of God, while in her own world of prayer, pouring out her heart to God, the man of God, Eli the priest, then accused her of being drunk. Can you imagine that? What could be more hurtful? In the middle of her sorrow, pouring her heart out to God, the priest incorrectly assumes she is intoxicated (1 Sam. 1:14). How much more humiliation could she endure?

Perhaps you are in a somewhat similar situation—you are unable to become pregnant; you are constantly mocked and laughed at by perhaps those closest to you, maybe family members. I too have been down this road of taunts and mocking. When I was born again, someone very close to me constantly make snide remarks about my faith. This hurt me, and all I could do was ask God not to let me be put to shame for trusting in Him and not let them have the last laugh. I held on to the promise of His Word, which says in Psalm 25:3, "Yea, let none that wait on thee be ashamed" (KJV).

Perhaps, like Hannah, you are constantly judged or mocked for things over which you have no control, and it seems like everyone hates you, and there is nothing you do that is pleasing. Rejoice! For the Lord your God is with you. Your prayers are about to be answered. Hannah perhaps thought that was it—that perhaps things could never get better since a priest in the house of God could not discern that she was in pain and greatly distressed. Rather, he saw her as a drunken woman who needed to get off the bottle. He condemned her "drunken state" right away. How many times have we all but given up on our faith in God because we do not understand His purposes? How many times have we thought, *No one understands me; no one cares*? How many times? Dear friend, God cares! God understands! And because He cares, He sent His only Son, Jesus, to die on the cross for you and me, just so that we can have abundant life. Just when we are about to give up, He shows up mightily. The fiery situations we find ourselves in or pass through help transform us and strengthen us inside, helping us become who God has always desired us to be.

After Hannah's deep communion in the place of prayer, God remembered her (1 Sam. 1:19). Transformation began right after. This once-sorrowful woman became a woman of faith, a woman who boldly entered into a covenant with the Lord, her Creator, who is a covenant-keeping God. She made a vow to the Lord (1 Sam. 1:11) and fulfilled that vow (1 Sam. 1:24–28). This transformation does not end here. Her language changed; it is prophetic in content (Sam. 2:1–10). She speaks boldly of this God she has come to know as merciful and faithful. She is not ashamed to declare His goodness and to tell of His salvation. This woman experienced a great deliverance from the oppression of the Enemy.

What are you holding on to? Is it fear? Are you afraid things will never work out for good for you? Let go, and let God work His perfect will in you. It is neither by might nor by power (Zech. 4:6; Eph. 2:8–9). Like the old gospel song says, "I owe it all to Jesus." We owe our salvation to our God. Hannah recognized and accepted this truth and sang about it. She could never have been in a position to tell it all, make vows, and fulfill them if transformation had not taken place in her life. In her trying times, Hannah found the grace to walk in humility, one of the marked signs of transformation. When God's power is at work in us, self dies and gives way to grace, and in our weakness, God's strength is made perfect (2 Cor. 12:9). Praise the Lord! So Hannah, after she had patiently endured, inherited the promise and blessings due her.

Mary Magdalene: What shall we say about Mary Magdalene, from whom seven demons were cast out? Demons, as we know, torment! That is one of their job descriptions, and their ultimate goal is to destroy totally. In the Bible, we see examples of how they operate. They inflict wounds, they try to destroy, they try to kill, they keep those they possess in a totally depressed state, and they manifest violence in the lives of those they are tormenting.

In the New Testament, we see the father of a young boy possessed by demons; he comes to Jesus for help. "Teacher, I brought my son for you to heal—he can't talk because he is possessed by a demon. And whenever the demon is in control of him it dashes him to the ground and makes him foam at the mouth and grind His teeth and become rigid" (Mark 9:17–18 LB). The boy was brought to Jesus, but when the demon saw Him, it "convulsed the child horribly, and he fell to the ground writhing and foaming at the mouth" (Mark 9:20). Demons want control! In the Amplified Bible, it says, "It lays hold of him [so as to make him its own]" (Mark 9:18). Satan wants to control us, God's children! Not only that but we see that the demon that possessed this boy did not stop at dashing him to the ground. It also "often makes him fall into the fire or water to kill him" (Mark 9:22 LB). The King James Version says the demon wants "to destroy" the boy. This demon was truly bent on killing this boy. The ultimate goal of demons is to kill, as we can see. They steal (people's joy, peace, strength, you name it), they kill, and they aim at destroying (John 10:10).

A mother from Canaan tells Jesus that her daughter is "grievously vexed with a devil" (Matt. 15:22 KJV). *The Living Bible* says "it torments her constantly," meaning that the demon did nothing but torment this girl continuously. In Mark 5, we see a man in a similar situation, tormented continually: "all day long and through the night he would wander among the tombs and in the wild hills, screaming and cutting himself with sharp pieces of stone" (v. 5 LB).

Is the tomb a place in which to live, twenty-four/seven? I think not! But here was a man who found himself in that situation and not because he chose to be in it. He was cutting himself with sharp pieces of stone, screaming and crying. Is this not torment? Where is the joy in cutting oneself, screaming and crying? Where is the rest in this kind of situation? This man could find no rest, no joy, and no peace in his condition. He was often bound with chains (to keep him from hurting himself and others, I guess), yet he often broke free of those chains—that's the strength of demons manifested right there. Demons are somewhat powerful and numerous. This man, we are told, had a "legion" inside of him (a Roman legion had up to six thousand soldiers). Are we surprised, then, that he was able to break free from the chains used to hold him down? We are further told that when the legion of demons was cast out of this man, they asked him if they could enter a herd of swine close by. Jesus sent them into the herd of swine, and they caused the herd (nearly two thousand of them) to run violently down a steep place and were choked in the sea. All seven sons of Sceva, a chief priest, were overpowered and wounded by one man possessed by a demon (Acts 19:14–16).

There are many more instances in the Bible of people tormented or afflicted by evil or unclean spirits (demons). The examples that have been highlighted here are not for the purpose of scaring you but for you to imagine how life must have been for Mary Magdalene before the seven demons were cast out of her. Here she was, delivered and set free from the oppression of the demons. So what possible transformation could she have undergone? I'll show you! Before deliverance came for her, she was in no position to truly understand and appreciate life and the joys of living. The demons were controlling her life, thereby making her as miserable as possible, because they tormented her continually. Demons love to inhabit bodies. Jesus said about demon possession,

> "If the demon leaves, it goes into the deserts for a while, seeking rest, but finding none. Then it says, 'I will return to the man I came from.' So it returns and finds the man's heart clean but empty! Then the demon finds seven other spirits more evil than itself, and all enter the man and live in him. And so he is worse off than before" (Matt. 12:43–45 LB).

Remember I said earlier that tormenting is part of a demon's job description. And looking at the examples given earlier of people afflicted or tormented by demons, you can now understand what bad shape Mary Magdalene's life was in before Jesus came into it. She needed help and needed it desperately. Because demons cause depression, this woman was probably sad most of the time. She no doubt had sleepless nights from depression and worried about her state of mind. She probably experienced mood swings all the time; had fear in her heart, not knowing what the day would bring for her or what she would do to herself; and perhaps was in constant pain because of wounds she may have tried to inflict on herself, perhaps while trying to commit suicide. Unlike King Saul, she did not have a "David" to play on the harp for her so that the demons would leave (1 Sam. 16:23). We can only imagine what life must have been for her, and I can sum it up for you in one word: *hell!*

If a person has not been down a road like May Magdalene's, then he or she sure would not understand the very miserable life she was living. I can relate to her frame of mind in a way because there was a time in my life when I could not figure out why I was depressed and so easily discouraged for no reason at all. There was even a time when I thought my time on earth was up. I had negative thoughts of putting things in place for my husband and children so that they would not have to look for things after I was gone. Thoughts such as these came into my heart repeatedly. This was a sentence of death that the Enemy had brought upon me to oppress me and make me give up on the life God had given me. Paul said, "Indeed, we felt within ourselves that we had received the [very] *sentence of death*" (2 Cor. 1:9 AB, emphasis added).

God, in His great love and mercy, broke through for me and set me free through the power of His Spirit and in His Son's name. Deliverance came for me, just as I know that it can come for you, through Jesus

Christ. And today, I am free in Christ and enjoying the power of the Holy Spirit working in me.

The same grace that brought me through those years is available for you today. Just call on the name of Jesus, and He will answer you. He is waiting; call on Him. Don't hesitate, for the Bible tells us that "whosoever [and that includes you] shall call on the name of the Lord shall be delivered" (Joel 2:32 KJV). Mary Magdalene's deliverance from demons came from the Lord Himself and not of her own self or making. He brought peace to her soul. She began living again, as God had ordained her life should be. Having tasted of the Lord's goodness and having seen His mercies in her life, she chose to stick close to the Lord. She walked with Him and followed His ministry closely, learning from Him (Luke 8:1–2). We see her near the cross at Jesus's crucifixion (John 19:25); she was also at His burial (Matt. 27:61), and she was there at the tomb first thing on Sunday morning and was the one to whom Jesus appeared first after His resurrection and not His disciples (Mark 16:9). This was all because He found her faithful. Her love for Him was real! Like Mary, Jesus's mother, she had tasted of the Lord's goodness and concluded that He is good (Ps. 34:8), and she chose to stay close to Him. Jesus knew He could trust her, and she knew that her Savior was trustworthy and worth staying close to.

During her close walk with Jesus before His death, Mary allowed His words to have a place in her heart, hiding them in her heart and allowing the words He spoke to cleanse her. The words of the psalmist in Psalm 119:11—"Thy word have I hid in mine heart, that I might not sin against thee" (KJV)—are May Magdalene's sentiments exactly. She loved her Lord so much because she knew where she had been, what her life had been, and what she had become in Him because of Him. This was why after Jesus's death, she went very early to the tomb, because she missed Him, and she could not bear the thought of being separated from Him. This was selfless love in action. When you walk closely with the Lord, you grow to love Him more and more, and you are more than willing to give up all for Him. So why don't you taste and see His goodness work in your life? Mary Magdalene became a worshipper because of the transformation she underwent.

Esther: Esther too experienced a transforming process in her life. Her transformation story was from living the life of a peasant girl to living life as a queen. She learned how to walk in humility, grace, wisdom, and faith. She learned to take her eyes off herself and put others first (Est. 4:16). She, who once walked in fear after becoming queen (Est. 4:11), became bold as a lion. Through faith and trusting in God, she obtained favor from the king and used that favor to walk in wisdom for and on behalf of her people, the Jews.

What about you? Don't sell yourself short! What are the things you think you can't do that are impossible? I would say practically nothing, really, because God's Word says, "For I can do everything God asks me to with the help of Christ who gives me the strength and power" (Phil. 4:13 LB). It is through the grace of God and the power of the Holy Spirit that anyone is able to accomplish anything in life. So stop beating yourself up and allowing the Enemy to tell you what you can and cannot do. It is not by our own power or ability; it is with the help of the Holy Spirit. Remember that what is impossible with you is possible with God (Matt. 19:26).

Rahab: What a woman! Little is known of this woman and her background, except that she was a pagan and a prostitute. Before her transformation, Rahab was her own woman, in control of her surroundings. She did what she wanted, when she wanted, and however she wanted. Not even the king of Jericho could make her do what she did not want to do (Josh. 2:2–4).

Rahab was also a woman who was very much aware of what was

going on around her. She was not ignorant at all. Read what she said to the spies sent by Joshua,

> "I know perfectly well that your God is going to give my country to you … We are all afraid of you; everyone is terrified if the word Israel is even mentioned. For we have heard how the Lord made a path through the Red Sea for you when you left Egypt! And we know what you did to Sihon and Og, the two Amorite kings east of the Jordan, and how you ruined their land and completely destroyed their people. No wonder we are afraid of you! No one has any fight left in him after hearing things like that, for your God is the supreme God of heaven, not just an ordinary god" (Josh. 2:9–11 LB).

This woman was a harlot (a prostitute), yet she did not let her way of living keep her in the dark. The book of Proverbs highlights a couple of words we could use to describe the character and person of one who is or is seen as a harlot: "evil woman," "loose woman" (6:24 AB), "strange woman" (7:5 KJV), a woman with "flattering lips" (7:21 KJV). "For on account of a harlot a man is brought to a piece of bread, and the adulteress stalks and snares [as with a hook] the precious life [of a man]" (6:26 AB). She is "sly and cunning of heart" (7:10 AB), "loud and stubborn" (7:11 KJV), always lying in wait (setting ambushes to seduce men), and deceptive in her ways and dealings with people. "She has cast down many wounded, and all who were slain by her were strong men" (Prov. 7:26 NKJV). In effect, a harlot is a big-time seductress (Prov. 7:16–20; 9:14–15). This is how strong a personality a harlot has—overwhelming control. Wow! And Rahab was a harlot? What a life! What a lifestyle! And not a healthy lifestyle, I should say! Yet Rahab lived this lifestyle for God knows how long. She was a woman with all the odds against her because of her character and lifestyle, yet God, in His infinite wisdom and mercy, chose her and worked a marvelous work in her life. And through His divine plan, she became an ancestress of David and of Jesus Christ (Matt. 1:5). Indeed, "God shows no partiality" (Acts 10:34).

Perhaps reading all of these terrible character traits reminds you of your present lifestyle, and you are wondering when you will ever get out of it. Be encouraged! The same God who delivered Rahab out of her horrible lifestyle is able to deliver you. Impossible situations are God's specialty. The three Hebrew boys who were thrown into the fiery furnace by the wicked King Nebuchadnezzar dared to believe God for their deliverance. Read what they said in their difficult situation: "If we are thrown into the flaming furnace, *our God is able to deliver us; and he will deliver us* out of your hand, Your Majesty" (Dan. 3:17 LB, emphasis added).

I want you to know that God has definite plans for you, just as He had plans for Rahab, and in His mercy He will fulfill His divine plans for your life because He is God, and He alone works in us, both to will and to do of His good pleasure (Phil. 2:13).

The Life of the Harlot Rahab

Now let us try to imagine a day in the life of Rahab. She gets up every morning with one goal in mind: to seduce and have sexual relations with both the unsuspecting man (perhaps one who was new in town) and the one who was willing to just enjoy the pleasure of sin for a moment. She sets out each new day, trying to make as much money as possible. For all we know, she may have been running a brothel, but we are told that she was a harlot and that the two spies Joshua sent to Jericho went to her house and lodged there (Josh. 2:1). Now, considering the times in which Rahab lived, being involved in random sexual activities without the use of any form of protection whatsoever exposed her to all kinds of venereal diseases. She was basically practicing unsafe sex. Who knows how many times she may have gotten pregnant and how many times she got rid of pregnancies? Who knows how many times she may have had sexually transmitted diseases? God alone knew, and it did not stop Him from loving her dearly.

As I write this, I sense there is someone reading this who is sad because he or she has walked a similar path, and he or she is full of regrets. Listen, before you continue beating yourself up, know this: God alone is perfect, and He loves, is forgiving, and is full of compassion. His Word says, "If we confess our sins, He is faithful and just to forgive us our sins and to cleanse us from all unrighteousness" (1 John 1:9 NKJV). Proverbs 28:13 says, "A man who refuses to admit his mistakes can never be successful. But if he confesses and forsakes them, he gets another chance" (LB), or as the King James Version puts it, "Whoso confesseth and forsaketh [his sins] them shall have mercy"—mercy from God the Father. So why not go ahead and receive the mercy from God that is waiting for you? All you have to do is confess your sins to Him, and accept His love and forgiveness. You do not have to remain in that state of condemnation all your life. Remember that Rahab's lifestyle did not stop God from loving her, and He gave her a future and a hope.

I have wondered how and why Rahab got involved in such an ugly business. Perhaps it was out of frustration, maybe rejection, or maybe because life had thrown her a couple of curve balls. Whatever it was that led her into that lifestyle, it was not God's will for her. It certainly could not have been a happy lifestyle, even if she had put up appearances for people. Rahab would have suffered a lot of emotional and physical abuse from almost all, if not all, the men who came to her. Each day must have been like hell for her, especially not knowing how badly she would be treated by each client. Maybe as a result of these kinds of abusive treatments, she decided to become hardened emotionally and to live out the full meaning of her name: "proud, boastful." Walking pridefully and ignoring the ugly reality of her life must have somehow kept her going every day.

I imagine there must have been days when Rahab felt like giving up on this kind of life, but because she thought she had an edge over other women (e.g., she was her own woman who could go and come as she pleased, and she had a house on the wall of Jericho with a great view), she did not quit. Maybe she felt she could do nothing else to earn a living if she got out of that lifestyle, or maybe she was thinking like you might be thinking now as you read this—already feeling judged and condemned and saying, "I am so deep into this kind of dirty lifestyle that there is no way out."

Wait a minute! Don't say that! This is where you are wrong. There is hope for the hopeless, even now, right this moment, in Christ Jesus. For God uses every temptation or setback in our lives to make a way of escape for us. This again is one of the main reasons why Christ came: to turn the sinner to repentance and also to give each and every one of us abundant life in Him. Jesus said, "They that are whole have no need of the physician, but they that are sick: I came not to call the righteous, but sinners to repentance" (Mark 2:17 KJV).

Do you qualify for this abundant life promised to you? The answer is yes. So please do not hold on to the thought that there is no way out for you or that nobody else will want to have anything to do with you because of the way you have lived your life. Rahab chose to live the life of a prostitute, but God, in His infinite wisdom and mercy, had other plans for her life. Even before she was born, God Himself had destined greatness for her life, just as He has destined greatness for you. God had already made a way of escape for Rahab, and He practically guided her into the way He had made for her. How? Because she was a common prostitute, the men who came around her probably had a lot of discussions with her about practically everything. They might have told her intimate things, such as their fears (perhaps some soldiers came around her as well), and she, being a smart woman, would have paid close attention to what was being discussed. She could have known more about the city's national security than most of the men and women in Jericho because of her lifestyle. So from those close encounters with the men of the city, she would have begun to understand that there was a people who lived outside Jericho whose God was all-powerful and fought for His own and gave them great victories. What she might have heard from these men would have intrigued her and, of course, aroused her curiosity about this God and His people, the children of Israel. Why? Because she could not understand how men in a *walled city* such as Jericho were given to such visible fear.

Read her words to the spies in Joshua 2:9–11: "All the inhabitants of the land faint because of you … And as soon as we had heard … our hearts did melt, neither did there remain any more courage in any man, because of you" (KJV). God used all of this going on around Rahab to begin to stir in her heart a yearning for Him. So when the opportunity came for her to experience this God for herself, she took it, and through faith she too inherited her promise. "By faith—because she believed in God and His power—Rahab the harlot did not die with all the others in her city when they refused to obey God, for she gave a friendly welcome to the spies" (Heb. 11:31 LB). For Rahab to fully inherit her blessings from God and to walk in His salvation plan for her life, she had to do away with her old way of living and embrace a new and healthy lifestyle. In other words, she had to totally walk away from prostitution, a lifestyle she had come to embrace for God knows how long.

She began this journey into her new life by first accepting God's plan for her life—Christ's finished work on the cross at Calvary, His shed blood, which is symbolically represented in Rahab's story by the scarlet rope she hung out of her window, indicating to the Israelites that she and her family were to be spared (Josh. 2:17–21). By hanging that scarlet rope out of her window, Rahab was declaring openly her acceptance of God's love and His grace and mercy toward her, and she, in return, extended the same to her family. God does not give us His love and extend mercy and grace to us just for us. He expects us to give to others just as freely as He has given to us. "Freely (without pay) you have received, freely (without charge) give" (Matt. 10:8 AB). Rahab, having begun to experience and enjoy a new way of living and knowing what she knew (what was about to happen to her city), could not sit back and let her family perish. She had to do something and do it fast, because she did not know what hour the spies would be returning with the armies of Israel to take Jericho. So what did she do? She stepped out in faith again, this time extending God's love to her family. She invited them to stay with her in her house.

For all we know, her relationship with them may not have been the best because of the life she was living, but she cared enough for their salvation and deliverance. She did not let any differences between them stop her. So also we should not allow contentions from our past stop us from showing God's love to anyone who might need it. The greatest gift of all is love.

> "Love is very patient and kind, never jealous or envious,
> never boastful or proud, never haughty or selfish or rude.

Love does not demand its own way. It is not irritable or touchy. It does not hold grudges and will hardly even notice when others do it wrong. It is never glad about injustice, but rejoices whenever truth wins out. If you love someone, you will be loyal to him no matter what the cost. You will always believe in him, always expect the best of him, and always stand your ground in defending him" (1 Cor. 13:4–7 LB).

Love goes on forever!

Rahab lived the Word in 1 Corinthians 13, having invited her family to come live with her while awaiting the attack on the city of Jericho. It could not have been easy being patient or kind with all the people in her house. In addition to housing the family, Rahab also had to feed them. Imagine what the living situation must have been for all of them, especially for her. No more privacy, no more quiet in her home when she wanted it, and no going out of the house for a breath of fresh air or to get away from anyone—she was warned by the spies that if anyone was outside her home when the attack on Jericho happened, that individual would not be spared. But she was a determined woman, determined to live for this God she had heard so much about (the God the men of Jericho feared) and the one to whom she had come to surrender her life, determined to know Him, determined to be a part of His people. By tolerating and accommodating all the people in her house during this waiting period, Rahab demonstrated that she was willing to pay the price of dying to her selfish ways of doing things. She had come to understand that it was no longer about her living for herself, but it was about her agreeing with God's plan for her life and aligning herself with that purpose, just so that God's kingdom would come and so that His will would be done on earth as it is in heaven.

What if she had not aligned herself with the will of God? It is possible that she could have been killed, alongside her family. Further, the heritage of being in the lineage of Christ could have been eliminated for Rahab and her descendants. This is why it is important that you and I understand that everything is not about us but about God, about His will, about His purpose, and about His kingdom! His will, not ours! Before we proceed any further, I want us to pause and appreciate the work God's grace and mercy did in Rahab's life.

Her faith in this God of the children of Israel, whom she had heard so much about, whom she was yet to get to know for herself, made her whole. God responds to faith. Hebrews 11 tells us that Rahab "through faith … obtained promises" (Heb. 11:31, 33 KJV).

Wouldn't you agree that Rahab started her faith journey on a good note? She stepped out in faith, believing that "the Lord your God, He is God in heaven above, and in earth beneath" (Josh. 2:10 KJV), and of course this pleased God. "But without faith it is impossible to please … [God]. For whoever would come near to God must [necessarily] believe that God exists" (Heb.11:6 AB, emphasis added). Or as the King James Version says, "He that cometh to God must believe that He is" (emphasis added). God is the same yesterday, today, and forever! Hallelujah!

God and God alone made it possible for Rahab to receive her entire family into her home. And guess what? It was not just for a night or for a day, but it was for an indefinite period of time, because the spies never told her when they would be back to take Jericho. All they said to her regarding their invasion was, "Behold, when we come into the land" (Josh. 2:18 KJV). Rahab could not do much, considering the situation she was in. But through the grace of God at work in her life, I imagine she was able to love her family, be patient with them, and live in peace with them. She was living out James 5:7. "So be patient … [as you wait] till the coming of the Lord. See how the farmer waits expectantly for the precious harvest from the land. [See how] he keeps up his patient [vigil]" (AB).

Rahab waited patiently, establishing her heart for the coming of the Lord. Are you doing the same? The Bible says we do not know what hour He will come back (Matt. 24:36). The power of God works wonders continuously in a person's life. So why not let His power go to work in your life? You will be surprised at the new you. God has a plan and a great future for you.

Chapter 5

THE PROVERBS 31 WOMAN: CHARACTERISTICS OF THE TRANSFORMED WOMAN

But be thou an example of the believers, in word, in conversation, in charity, in spirit, in faith, in purity.
—1 TIMOTHY 4:12 (KJV)

This chapter is not about the portrayal of self. It is about instructions in righteousness, wisdom, the fear of God, being a blessing, putting others first, and caring about others, especially the poor and the helpless. It is also a reminder about endeavoring to fulfill your destiny, remembering God's Word implanted in your life, and using it wisely for God's kingdom. It's about what to do with your God-given life.

Each and every one of us has a purpose in life. What we do with our lives matters a lot to God. We are not to live for ourselves; we are to live for Him. For His purpose: "For thou hast created all things, and for thy pleasure they are and were created" (Rev. 4:11 KJV). We all need His presence in our lives to enable us to fulfill our destinies here on earth.

In the beginning of Proverbs 31, we are introduced to the wise counsel of King Lemuel's mother, a woman who must have experienced divine encounters at some point in her life because her words to her son give her away. We see divine wisdom, instructions in the fear of the Lord, and life and health in the words that she speaks to her son. And as we examine her words, we will see some wonderful character traits highlighted, the first being righteousness. King Lemuel's mother must have walked in righteousness to have been able to instruct her son in righteousness and in the fear of the Lord. Why? Because you cannot give away what you do not have. The beauty of this is that her son remembered his mother's instructions years later. As Proverbs says, "Train up a child in the way he should go: and when he is old, he will not depart from it" (22:6 KJV). Here we have a woman who taught her son the Word of God, and years later, here he is, remembering what he was taught. From a child, King Lemuel was *dedicated* to the Lord by his mother ("O my son, whom I have dedicated to the Lord" [31:2 LB, emphasis added]). Hannah, in 1 Samuel, and Mary, the mother of Jesus, are a couple of examples of women who dedicated their children to the Lord at very early ages.

Point One: *A transformed woman knows the importance of dedicating her children to the Lord.* And she does this by faith in God because she believes God, that He is able to preserve and protect whatever is committed into His hands for safekeeping (2 Tim. 1:12). She takes Him at His word. Proverbs 22:6 tells us that a child taught in the way of the Lord will not depart from it when he grows up.

Point Two: *A transformed woman is a teacher of God's Word.* Because she has been taught line upon line, precept upon precept, a little here and a little there by the Holy Spirit of God from the Word of God, the transformed woman is able to take the time to teach the Word of God to her children on a daily basis, rightly dividing the Word of truth (Heb. 4:12). She instructs them in righteousness with divine wisdom and what it means to walk in the fear of the Lord, because she knows that she is accountable to God for the children He has given to her. She is a dedicated mother! King Lemuel's mother, we see, was patient to highlight certain ways that would be destructive to her son's life if he followed those paths (see Proverbs 31: 3–5).

Point Three: *A transformed woman is not careless in her ways.* If anything, she is thorough in her ways, paying close attention to lifestyles or ways of doing things that might lead her children away from God and emphasizing those destructive ways to her children repeatedly. Why? Because she is determined to see her children fulfill their destinies in Christ.

King Lemuel's mother desired her son to fulfill his destiny as king, hence her counsel to him in Proverbs 31:3.

Point Four: *A transformed woman is a crusader for Christ.* She is always willing to help the helpless and stand up for the poor. She sees every soul as precious, to be helped and encouraged and not ignored. She reaches out in love and tries to help whatever need the poor might have, to the best of her ability. "Are you called to help others? Do it with all the strength and energy that God supplies so that God will be glorified through Jesus Christ" (1 Peter 4:11 LB).

Point Five: *A transformed woman is humble, recognizing that she is who she is because of God's grace on her life.* She is always quick to give God the glory because she knows that "grace and truth came by Jesus Christ" (John 1:17 KJV). The transformed woman walks in humility, serves in humility, and loves easily, all because she has passed through God's refining fire. Passing through God's refining fire builds character. The transformed woman who has passed through God's refining fire can be trusted. Proverbs 31:11 says "the heart of her husband doth safely trust in her" (KJV). Her husband relies on and believes in her securely; others around her trust her and feel safe and confident around her. This woman is truly a helpmeet (Gen. 2:18), an encouragement, and a comfort to her husband.

Point Six: *A transformed woman is strong.* Because of the power of God at work in her life, this woman is no longer lazy. She is energetic, a hard worker, and full of dignity. She works hard every single day, taking good care of the home front and business.

Point Seven: *A transformed woman is very considerate.* She lives to give and help others. "She sews for the poor and generously helps those in need" (Prov. 31:19-20 LB). The word "generously" clearly denotes the extent to which this woman would go to do anything for anybody. It clearly describes how openhanded she is; one given to giving without hesitation and without reservation! What a generous heart! God loves a cheerful giver (2 Cor. 9:7). What about you? When we learn to give of ourselves to help or bless others, Jesus is glorified, and our joy is full. And the woman who is experiencing God's love and the power of His forgiveness knows this to be very true. For giving is God's nature, and the Bible tells us that He "*so loved the world, that he gave* his only begotten Son" (John 3:16 KJV, emphasis added).

Point Eight: *A transformed woman is careful in her ways.* She is careful to avoid the pitfalls of life—the *how, what, where,* and *who* that lead people away from God. She is discerning and bold; fear has no place in her life and neither has deception. She lives by the truth of God's Word and is a blessing to her family and to all spiritually. She is a woman who is praised by her husband, by her children, and by all who know her. Also, because she has passed through God's refining fire and has come out as pure gold (Job 23:10; 1 Peter 1:7), she is passionate about seeing people fulfill their destiny in Christ. She knows the importance of walking in and fulfilling one's destiny because she has been on that road. She knows that God is a God of purpose and that timing is everything with Him. She also knows that if people are not careful, they could miss God. A lazy mind and an undiscerning heart could very easily miss out on what God has in store.

The children of Issachar were men who had understanding of the times and the season to know what they were supposed to do (1 Chron. 12:32). A woman who has experienced God's power of transformation in her life—because she knows that time is of the essence—encourages others to spend their time here on earth wisely. "And if ye call on the Father, who without respect of persons judgeth according to every man's work, pass *the time* of your sojourning here in fear" (1 Peter 1:17 KJV, emphasis added). King Lemuel's mother had understanding and shared this truth (the importance of spending one's time wisely here on earth) with her son by encouraging him not to waste his time on women and on the things that destroyed kings. In Hebrews 10:24–25, it is written, "And let us consider one another to provoke unto love and to good works: Not forsaking the assembling of ourselves together, as the manner of some is; but exhorting one another: and so much the more, as ye see the day approaching" (KJV). In other words, manage your time wisely; do what you know you should be doing, and do it diligently!

Point Ten: *A transformed woman is valuable to God and others as well.* In other words, she is very dear and precious to all who know her because she is considerate of others. Her generosity and willingness to help others knows no bounds; she is hardworking, discerning, and careful in her ways. "Her price is far above rubies" (Prov. 31:10 KJV), meaning that she is worth more than precious gems. We see also that her relationship with the Lord is very important and precious to her.

She "fears and reverences God" (Prov. 31:30 LB), or as the Amplified Bible puts it, she is a woman who "reverently and worshipfully fears the Lord."

"A capable, intelligent and virtuous woman—who is he who can find her?" (Prov. 31:10 AB). Answer? The Lord alone: "a wise, understanding, and prudent wife is from the Lord" (Prov. 19:14 AB).

The Lord is the one who perfects us. So do not be discouraged about your life. God wants to transform you into the image of His likeness, to perfect that which concerns you. It is what He has been longing to do for you so that eventually you will be with Him in His heavenly kingdom, just as Jesus said to the thief on the cross: "Today you will be with me in Paradise. This is a solemn promise" (Luke 23:43 LB).

In conclusion, I encourage you to renew your mind daily with the Word of God, yield to the Holy Spirit, and obey His instructions. Let Him teach you and help you walk on this journey called life, and you will see definite changes take place in your life, for Jesus Christ is Lord!

Chapter 6

THE LANGUAGE OF A TRANSFORMED WOMAN: THE SONG OF THE REDEEMED

Hear; for I will speak of excellent things; and the
opening of my lips shall be right things.
—PROVERBS 8:6 (KJV)

When we talk about language, what do we really mean? Language is really man's means of communication (the words we speak or say to one another). While trying to write this chapter, when I looked into the Scriptures I was amazed at how many Scriptures kept leaping off the pages of the Bible at me and giving me a better understanding how the very words that we speak or confess to one another or before God are important. They could mold our lives for good or bad. The words we choose to release from our mouths make all the difference.

I do read my Bible every day—don't get me wrong now—but seeing some of these Scriptures in a new light (the eyes of my understanding were being enlightened, so to speak) caused me to marvel at the depth and the power in every God-breathed word. As I began to ponder and go through some of these Scriptures, I found myself searching my heart, weighing my language (especially in light of Proverbs 8:6, above), and I wondered if I *truly have been speaking excellent things.* Each time I opened my lips to speak, did the right words come out of my mouth? I realized that I had fallen short; I had missed it so many times! This was really disheartening.

You know, we all say a lot of things each day, but we are unaware of how the words we speak, in excitement, depression, or anger, produce a negative influence on the hearers, causing them to become someone other than who God has called and destined them to be. Some people talk fast; some are slow talkers; some stammer; some just love to talk dirty (you don't want to be around such people); some do nothing but constantly use abusive words whenever they open their mouths; some people are just soft-spoken; some are so full of God's love it just oozes out as they speak; and some weigh their words before they speak.

James 1:19 commands us to "be swift to hear, *slow to speak*" (KJV, emphasis added). In other words, don't just open your mouth to speak carelessly, but speak with the wisdom of God, and let what you say be the right thing. I could go on and on about the way people speak (though this is not all about how fast or how slow people talk), but the truth is that unless the Word of God richly dwells in each and every one of us, much of what we say on a daily basis will just be mere words, which "go in one ear and out the other" (Prov. 29:19 MSG). The Bible says we should have "truth in [our] inward parts" (Ps. 51:6 NKJV), because "out of the abundance of the heart the mouth speaks" (Matt 12:34 NLJV). God wants us to live rich, healthy lives, and when we speak God's language of love, we find ourselves blessing one another in love, and our lives become healthy, and God is glorified. Bottom line: what we say and how we say it are important to God.

Proverbs 25:11 says, "A word fitly spoken is like apples of gold in settings of silver" (NKJV). "A word spoken at the right moment—how good it is!" (Prov.15:23 AB). Did you get that? How the word spoken at the right time can be refreshing and a blessing? This truly is what a lot of believers struggle with, getting themselves to say the right thing at the right time. So when we say the wrong things at the wrong time, our words not only snare others, but we also become ensnared by what we have spoken (Prov. 6:2). Little wonder the psalmist prayed, "Let the words of my mouth, and the meditation of my heart, be acceptable in thy sight, O lord, my strength, and my redeemer" (Ps. 19:14 KJV).

You can tell a person's beliefs or the principles by which he or she lives by the things he or she says. People's speech gives them away so easily. The Bible tells us that death and life are in the power of the tongue, and whatever we say we will eat the fruit thereof (Prov. 18:21). Words control destinies, and whatever we say will transport us to the very places of which we have spoken easily. So why are some of us believers still speaking the language of the world (e.g., deceit, cursing, faithlessness, exaggeration, foolishness, covetousness, fear, criticism, seduction, murmuring, blasphemy), despite the fact that we have been redeemed by the precious blood of Christ? My belief is this: we have not truly learned how to order our conversation aright, and so we limit God from moving powerfully for and on our behalf (see Psalm 50:23).

Psalm 34:1 says, "I will bless the Lord at all times: his praise shall continually be in my mouth" (KJV). This, dear friend, is what our language is supposed to be—the language of praise and blessing. No wonder the Bible encourages us to bless even those who curse us (see Matthew 5:44 and Romans 12:14). Now let us closely examine the language of the women mentioned in the earlier chapters of this book. We begin again with Mary, the mother of Jesus. In Luke 1:30–31, we see the angel Gabriel has just told Mary that she is going to give birth to the Son of God, and her response to that is with honesty, holy fear, purity, and simplicity of heart. Read her words: "How shall this be, seeing I know not a man?" (Luke 1:34 KJV). *The Living Bible* translation puts it this way: "But how can I have a baby? I am a virgin." The angel Gabriel then tells her how the Word of God was going to come to pass, and so with godly fear and reverence, she responds, "I am the Lord's servant, and I am willing to do whatever he wants. May everything you said come true" (Luke 1:38 LB). In this instance, we see Mary opening her mouth with wisdom, knowledge, and understanding as she magnifies the Lord (see Proverbs 31:26) and declaring with humility her submission to the will of God for her life.

After the departure of the angel Gabriel, we see Mary again saying something. This time her language is the language of praise. She magnifies the Lord with all that is within her (Ps. 103:1). "And Mary said, my soul magnifies and extols the Lord, And my spirit rejoices in God my Savior" (Luke 1:46–47 AB).And she goes on and on, extolling the goodness, faithfulness, mercy, and greatness of God, now referred to as "the Magnificat," or "Mary's Song of Praise":

My soul magnifies the Lord,

and my spirit rejoices in God my Savior,

for He has looked with favor on the lowliness of His servant.

Surely, from now on all generations will call me blessed;

for the Mighty One has done great things for me, and holy is His name.

His mercy is for those who fear Him from generation to generation.
He has shown strength with His arm;
He has scattered the proud in the thoughts of their hearts.
He has brought down the powerful from their
thrones, and lifted up the lowly;
He has filled the hungry with good things, and sent the rich away empty.
He has helped his servant Israel, in remembrance of His mercy,
according to the promise He made to our ancestors,
to Abraham and to His descendants forever.
—Luke 1:47–55 (NRSV)

Now, let us take a closer look at each verse. When Mary spoke the words, "My soul magnifies the Lord and my spirit rejoices in God my Savior," we see her expressing out loud exactly what was going on inside of her. Her soul and her spirit were terribly excited and doing wonderful things—rejoicing, praising God, declaring He is Lord. She was confessing truths about God; she just could not contain herself.

When we are bubbling with the joy of the Lord on the inside, it comes pouring out of us like rivers of living water. Our language (the words we speak) tells it all (the excitement, the joy, the laughter—you name it). *The Message: The Bible in Contemporary Language* says, "I'm bursting with God-news; I'm dancing the song of my Savior God." So also, when we feel depressed or discouraged, our language is laced with sadness or negativity, for out of the abundance of the heart, the mouth speaks.

So what's in your heart? Anything that defiles, coming straight out of your heart and through your mouth, will not allow you to say boldly and confidently that the Lord is your helper and your God.

Mary had her eyes on the Lord, and because of that, she was able to see things clearly, understand them clearly, and confidently say of the Lord that He has done so many wonderful things: "He has looked with favor on the lowliness of his servant"; "He has shown strength with His arm"; "He has scattered the proud in the thoughts of their hearts"; "He has brought down the powerful from their thrones"; "He has filled the hungry with good things"; "He has helped His servant Israel." We see Mary saying, more than six times in ten verses, the words "He has," thereby recognizing God's ability, grace, mercy, and power and giving Him all the praise for it. Praise God!

How you see God's purpose for your life will help you order both language and conversation aright. When you understand whose you are and why He called you to be His very own, you will hardly ever talk from an ignorant point of view. Instead, you will find yourself speaking with divine wisdom, a boldness and authority, and having faith that can move mountains. Remember King David? What did he declare about the Lord in Psalm 91:2? David declared, "He alone is my refuge, my place of safety; He is my God, and I am trusting Him" (LB). Now if you are in His light, you will surely see light (experience an enlightening of your understanding). In Psalm 36:9, the New King James Version clearly states this. So how can you be in His light? Just keep your eyes on Him, and you will surely behold His beauty and His glory.

Still examining Mary's language, we see her frequently refer to God as "the Lord" and "God my Savior," giving a very clear and definite picture of this God she has come to reverentially fear and adore, the Almighty, with whom she has a personal relationship. She declares Him to be the "Mighty One," who alone is able to do great things. How you see God is how you will talk of Him. If you see Him as small and unable to help, then that is how you will always speak of Him. It is not that God needs us to make Him big; He is God all by Himself.

He created everything, whether visible to the naked eye or not (Col. 1:16). He is Creator God!

Now, do you see God as Lord? Do you see Him as God, your Savior? Do you see Him as the mighty one who has done great things and is still doing great things for you? As I said earlier, how you receive and see God is exactly how you will see and describe Him to all others and to yourself.

Anna, the prophetess in Luke 2:38, spoke of Jesus to all. We are told she "began thanking God and telling everyone in Jerusalem" that the Savior had arrived (LB). This kind of beautiful love language is only born of an intimate relationship with the Lord.

Mary had just had a wonderful encounter with the angel Gabriel, who had brought wonderful news her way. This good news became a source of strength, for all of a sudden she could *boldly* praise the Lord, declaring, in sum, that the Lord is her helper (Heb. 13:6). If your conversation is clean and ordered aright, you will be bold and confident to say—to all who care to listen—that the Lord is your helper and that fear has no place within your heart.

A Reason to Sing!

If I asked you for the meaning of the word sing, you would say it simply means to sing a song. And you would be correct. In the Hebrew language, the word for sing is *halal*, meaning "to speak praise; thank; celebrate; glory; boast or sing."[1] And in the Greek language, the word is *humneo*, meaning "to celebrate God in song."[2] Do you have a reason to sing? I believe you do! Now, let us look at the reasons for glorying in God and speaking praises to Him in the lives of these women.

---

[1] James Strong, *The New Strong's Expanded Dictionary of Bible Words* (T. Nelson, 2001).

[2] Ibid.

A Reason to Sing—Mary's Song

> for *He has looked with favor* on the lowliness of His servant …
> for *the Mighty One* has done great things for me …
> He *has shown strength* with his arm;
> He *has scattered the proud* …
> He *has brought down the powerful* from their
> thrones, and *lifted up the lowly*;
> He *has filled the hungry with good things* …
> He *has helped* his servant (emphasis added).

God is a promise keeper! Whatever He says He will do, He does! His Word He has magnified above His name. The Bible tells us that God is not man that He should lie (Num.23:19). He is truth! "He has helped his servant Israel … according to the promise He made to our ancestors, to Abraham and to his descendants forever," and we are the descendants of Abraham (Luke 1: 4–55).

I am excited to tell you that you too have a reason to sing as Mary did, because God is gracious to each and every one of us. I recognize that many people may not feel like singing or even want to sing. The reason you may not be singing out loud about God's goodness today may partly be because you have not taken the time to reflect on God's goodness to you, as Mary did, and also partly because you may have let fear into your heart to steal your confidence and faith in a loving God. Mary had more to say about God's goodness to her—trust me; we all do!

Take some time to reflect on God's goodness and mercies to you. As the hymnist Johnson Oatman Jr. wrote, "Count your blessings, name them one by one, and it will surprise you what the Lord hath done."

God is good to us; let us not deny that. Now do you see why your language should be nothing but positive in character? Count your blessings, and be thankful to God, for He is truly gracious to you. When you take the time to count your blessings, you will truly appreciate God's mercies and kindness to you. Seek Him, and you will find Him! Throughout the book of Psalms, we see words like "I will sing"; "I will say of the Lord"; "O sing unto the Lord"; "Bless the Lord"; and so on. Words such as these tell us the one saying them is making a deliberate effort not just to say something to the Lord but also to say something about the Lord. When you spend time pouring out your love on the Lord deliberately (in prayer, in praise, in worship, while driving, while washing the dishes, while shopping, or even while relaxing), before you know it, your language will change and will become one with the Lord, because God who inhabits the praises of His people will transform your language. Praise the Lord, for He is good! Today, make that effort and say of the Lord that He is your refuge and your fortress. Let your spirit and your soul rejoice in Him and magnify His holy name. Amen!

Mary declared that her soul was magnifying the Lord and her spirit was rejoicing in God, her Savior. What about you? What is your spirit doing now? Are you allowing your soul and your spirit to magnify the Lord and rejoice in Him, to run into His loving arms and find rest there for your soul? Or are you allowing your soul and your spirit to wallow in the fields of loneliness and the pits of depression? Let your soul arise and magnify the Lord. Learn to discern what your soul needs always (that joy and exuberance in the Lord, not a quick fix or alcohol.), and you will quickly find rest for your soul.

Jesus is the Prince of Peace. You call on Him, and He will answer you. How did Mary know that the Lord had looked on her lowly state with favor? Because she heard the Word of the Lord from the mouth of His messenger, the angel Gabriel, and she not only received it with thanksgiving, but she also believed every word. Remember faith comes by hearing and hearing by the Word of God (Rom. 10:17). How did she know that all generations would call her blessed? Because she saw God's promise to her through the eyes of faith; she chose to believe it and confessed it. Why could she confidently talk about the great things God had done for her? Because she had tasted and seen that God is good. Do you remember her life story in chapter 3 of this book? God will always give us a new song to sing if we will only let Him take the reins of our hearts. He will always give us a reason to sing and rejoice in Him.

Let your soul make God big in that situation or state you are in right now, and see what He will do for you. Your life will never be the same, and your language will not ever be laced with covetousness again (Heb. 13:5). Your strength will be renewed like the eagles. You will run and not be weary, and you will definitely have a skip in your walk (Isa. 40:31). And like *The Message* states, you will be "bursting with God-news and dancing the song of your Savior" (Luke 1:46). Go ahead; give Him a chance to show you how much He cares for you.

Mary's words were prophetic, full of faith, full of love, full of gratitude, full of thanksgiving, gentle, without hypocrisy, and full of truths and appreciation for her Savior. Each time she said something, it was always in line with God's will and purpose for her life, and this always created an atmosphere for God to work even more specially in her life. "Blessed be the Lord, the God of Israel; He came and set his people free" (Luke 1:68 MSG).

A Reason to Sing—Hannah's Song

Hannah said, my heart exults and triumphs in the Lord;
my horn (my strength) is lifted up in the Lord.

My mouth is no longer silent, for it is opened
wide ... because I rejoice in Your salvation.
There is none holy like the Lord, there is none besides you;
there is no Rock like our God. Talk no more so very proudly;
let not arrogance go forth from your mouth,
for the Lord is a God of knowledge,
and by Him actions are weighed ... The Lord slays and makes alive;
He brings down to Sheol and raises up. The Lord makes
poor and makes rich; He brings low and He lifts up.
He raises up the poor out of the dust and lifts
up the needy from the ash heap,
to make them sit with nobles and inherit the throne of glory.
For the pillars of the earth are the Lord's, and
He has set the world upon them.
He will guard the feet of his godly ones ... for
by strength shall no man prevail.
The adversaries of the Lord shall be broken to pieces;
against them will He thunder in heaven.
The Lord will judge [all peoples] to the ends of the earth;
and He will give strength to His king (King)
and exalt the power of his anointed (Anointed, His Christ).
—1 Samuel 2:1–10 (AB)

Hannah, as we will see, had lots of reasons to sing. We all still have reasons to sing—good reasons. At this point in 1 Samuel 2, we are introduced to a joy-filled, singing Hannah. What happened to her? What brought about this sudden change in her voice, in her language, and in her emotions? Why is she filled with such joy? After all, in 1 Samuel 1, we saw a very miserable Hannah, who was so depressed and distressed that nothing her husband did or said to her gave her joy. Her rival, her husband's other wife, mocked her endlessly about being barren. She even described herself pitifully to the man of God who interrupted her while she was praying in the temple because he thought that she was drunk: "I am a woman of a sorrowful spirit" (1 Sam. 1:15 KJV).

But God changed all that for her. He stepped into her world; He remembered her (1 Sam. 2:19) and granted her the desire of her heart. And when the time came for the fulfillment of God's manifold goodness to her to be seen, she gave birth to a son, whom she called Samuel because, according to her, "I asked him of the Lord" (1 Sam. 2:20).

Now, Hannah had earlier promised the Lord she would give Samuel to Him after he was weaned (1 Sam. 2:11). And the time came for her to fulfill that promise, and boy, did she come with gladness of heart and singing to fulfill that promise! She was in a state of exuberance; her mouth was saying exactly what was going on inside of her (just like Mary). Her mouth was filled with exceeding joy. She declared, without hesitation, without reservation, to all who cared to listen (just like Anna the prophetess did in Luke 2) the greatness, the wisdom, the power, the merciful kindness, the might, and ability of God.

This is exactly what an experiential encounter with the living God will do to you. His goodness will cause you to want to sing of His mercies forever. "I will sing of the mercies of the Lord for ever: with my mouth will I make known thy faithfulness to all generations" (Ps. 89:1 KJV). Hannah was doing just that in the temple, making known God's faithfulness with her mouth. You will discover that as you begin to experience divine encounters with the Lord, being shy and holding back from telling anyone about God's love and goodness in your life will no longer have a stranglehold over you, simply because

God's transforming power is awesome. It can transform even the vilest sinner, give boldness and courage to the insecure, and satisfy every hungry heart.

The words that come out of a person's mouth tell all that is going on inside of him or her. Hannah was not just singing any song. Her song was born from a place of experience; it was born out of a grateful heart. She had just experienced God's love and mercy on a whole new level; she had tasted and seen that God is good indeed, and, as such, she was more than willing to tell all who cared to hear her sing about His goodness. Like Mary, her heart also rejoiced in God, her Savior. "My heart *exults* and *triumphs* in the Lord" (emphasis added). The word "exults" means "rejoice; glory," while the word "triumph" means "jump for joy" or "shout for joy." Hannah's heart was doing all of these in the Lord at the same time. What a wonderful spiritual exercise!

Now, if you were experiencing the same kind of situation as Hannah, a situation that was constantly bringing such great sorrow and pain on you, and the Lord showed up, showed you mercy, and gave you the same kind of breakthrough and victory that He gave Hannah, you would not keep silent. You too would surely sing out loud, and you would give Him thanks with a grateful heart. Hannah recognized that her entire being was "in the Lord"—her rejoicing, her strength, her voice, her everything. Little wonder she refused to keep silent. She said, "My mouth is no longer silent, for it is opened wide." When God gives you a reason to sing, you just cannot keep quiet. Your mouth will surely be opened wide to sing.

But the question now is this: do you know where you are? Are you in the Lord? Are your strength and your rejoicing in Him, or are they in another source? Unless "the eyes of your understanding" are enlightened by the Spirit of God Himself (Eph. 1:18), everything about you and around you will seem ordinary and perhaps even meaningless.

Hannah, by faith through grace, chose to rejoice in the salvation of the Lord, and because of her rejoicing, all she could do was open her mouth and declare. And declare, she did—prophetically! Having now seen God from an entirely new and different perspective, Hannah began to declare the goodness, the holiness, and the sovereignty of God in such wonderful ways. She says of the Lord in her song that He is holy, that He alone is God, and that there is none besides Him. She then goes on to further describe God as all-knowing, without injustice, one with whom nothing is impossible, Comforter, the One who lifts us up when we are downcast, who gives strength to His children, and also the One who orders and protects the footsteps of His chosen ones. Hannah flowed in the language of the prophetic as never before. This was a far cry from the woman we encountered earlier on, who was being intimidated by another woman. God had now become more real to Hannah than ever before. He had given her a reason to sing—victory over her enemies. God had satisfied her mouth with glad tidings.

The excitement of knowing that God is for you should be seen by all around you. Just know that you are loved by the One who conquered death, and if He is for you, who then can be against you? (Rom. 8:31). Just think about this for a moment. Isn't it wonderful? Isn't this exciting? What a glorious thought! If this is not worth shouting and singing about, you tell me otherwise. Oh, the joys of knowing and experiencing His great love and mercy! I encourage you to find your place in Jesus Christ today. There is plenty of room for you in Him. You do not have to walk this earth alone and afraid. God is for you and not against you! When you have so much of the joy of the Lord inside of you, nothing will discourage you or even weigh you down. Why? Because you will find yourself continually declaring His Word in faith (because your faith is stronger). "And they have overcome (conquered) him by means of the blood of the Lamb and by the utterance of their testimony, for they did not love and cling to life even when faced with death" (Rev. 12:11 AB).

If you strongly believe you do not have any reason whatsoever to sing, then I must submit to you that you have allowed yourself to be caught up in the Devil's lie. He tries to seduce us all the time, and he wants us all to believe that God does not love us, and that He is not as faithful as we think He is. Remember the Bible tells us that the Devil is a liar and that he comes to steal, to kill, and to destroy (John 10:10). But Jesus has come so that we can have abundant life. In the book of Revelation, the Enemy of our souls is referred to as "that age-old serpent, who is called the Devil and Satan, he who is the seducer (deceiver) of all humanity the world over" (12:9 AB). The Devil wants us to reject God's salvation plan for us. Just think: God gave His only Son to die on the cross for you and me, just so that we can have eternal life. What a loving and gracious Father!

Now I say to you again that if this is not reason enough to sing, I don't know what is. Come on; let us rejoice in the salvation the Lord has given us, and let us be thankful for such great salvation! Remember that your life is not your own. Our lives, our testimonies, our relationships—everything about us—all have to do with God's eternal plans and purposes for us.

Hannah's language reflects her adoration for her God and King and also her knowledge and understanding of Him. She blessed the Lord and glorified Him with all that was within her (Ps. 103:1; Jer. 9:24). You too can have a heavenly language like Hannah or Mary—sweet and full of praises and thanksgiving for the Father's love. You know why? Because you are not as horrible a person as you think you are, "for you have been chosen by God himself—you are priests of the King, you are holy and pure, *you are God's very own*" (1 Peter 2:9 LB, emphasis added). From the foundation of the world, He chose you for

Himself (Eph. 1:4) and is not willing to give up on you because of any wrong choices you may have made.

A Reason to Sing—Miriam's Song

> "Sing to the Lord, for He has triumphed gloriously. The horse and rider have been drowned in the sea" (Ex. 15:21 LB).

In this portion of Scripture, we see Miriam, the sister of Moses and Aaron, with tambourine in hand, leading the women in victory dances (Ex. 15:20). While they danced, she sang this song. Earlier in this chapter, Moses and all the children of Israel (including Miriam) sang this song on a lengthier note. But now, we see Miriam singing just a short note. Short, yes, but they were powerful words because she sang with all that was within her. Psalm 103:1 says, "Bless the Lord, O my soul; and *all that is within me*, bless His holy name" (NKJV, emphasis added). This was not just any song for Miriam; it was a reminder of God's faithfulness, a reminder of what God had just done for Israel, and she did not want them forgetting it so soon. Every so often, we need to remind ourselves of God's faithfulness and sing about it. God loves to hear us singing, because as we sing to Him, He will rejoice over us with singing and great gladness (Zeph. 3:17).

God had just defeated the enemies of the children of Israel, the Egyptians. He drowned them in the sea right before the eyes of all Israel (Exodus 14). And because of this, Moses, Miriam, and all of Israel burst out singing and dancing before the Lord (Exodus 15).

Come on; what else do you think they could have done after witnessing such a great deliverance but to declare the wondrous works of God? If you were in their shoes, experiencing deliverance such as they did by the hand of God, you surely would sing, dance, shout, and worship God with all your might. I cannot emphasize this enough that we need to remind ourselves constantly, on a daily basis, of how great God is, how good He is to us, and how much He is willing to do for us. After all, He gave His only Son to die on the cross for us for our redemption. He is great, and He does wondrous things. He alone is God! (Ps. 86:10). Praise His holy name!

There is a story of a man who was born lame, who was daily laid at the gate of the temple called Beautiful to ask alms from everyone who went into the temple. He experienced a miracle from God, and what did he do? The Bible tells us that he went into the temple with Peter and John, walking and leaping and praising God (Acts 3:2–8). Just as I said earlier, you too would do the same thing—show and tell all who cared to hear and see you what the Lord had done for you.

Now, back to Miriam! Miriam paints a very vivid picture with her words. In her song, she declares again what the Lord has done. She did not want them forgetting so soon, and neither did she want them to offer just any praise. She wanted them to see and to understand that what God had just done for them was very huge. It was a big deal! God had done yet another miracle, something they least expected Him to do. When she said, "*Sing* to the Lord," she was *encouraging* them to keep on singing God's praise. Perhaps the enthusiasm in their voices was slowly giving way to tiredness. After all, they had walked all night through the length of the sea, while the Egyptians were riding on chariots in hot pursuit. Miriam knew that this was not the time to get tired. She, being a prophetess, knew the importance of timing. She had discerned weariness coming on the people. These were a people who had earlier offered exuberant worship to God. And now, they were growing a little weary.

Knowing that there is a right time for everything, what did Miriam do? She took a tambourine and led the women in dances

("There is a right time for everything … a time to dance" [Eccl. 3:4 LB]) and then commanded them to sing to the Lord! It was not an appeal; it was a command. We need to encourage one another to never stop praising the Lord and singing of His mercies. Throughout the book of Psalms, we see the word "sing." The Bible encourages us to sing to the Lord. Psalm 89:1 reads, "I will sing of the mercies of the Lord forever" (NKJV).

Right now, I am not talking about a sweet singing voice, because it does not matter if your voice is not fantastic. I am talking about true worship—worship that declares God's faithfulness to all, and as long as your worship, your praise, and your adoration to the King of Kings comes straight from your heart, that is all that counts—not worship out of a feigned heart. You know, there are times when people worship God or sing songs of praise and seem like they are truly worshiping God with all that is within them, but really, their hearts are so far away from God. With your mouth make known God's faithfulness to all generations. Remember God looks at a man's thoughts and intentions; that is, the heart! (1 Sam. 16:7).

Moses described God as having "triumphed gloriously" (Ex. 15:1). If you were asked today to describe all the victories God has given you in one word, how would you describe all of His acts and mercies to you? Whenever we declare God's wondrous works to one another, we encourage each other to trust in the living God—and trust me; God always shows up in a much bigger way than we expect when we do this, and He never forgets His own.

> Then those whose lives honored God got together and talked it over. God saw what they were doing and listened in. A book was opened in God's presence, and minutes were taken of the meeting, with the names of

the God-fearers written down—all the names of those who honored God's name. God of the Angel Armies said, "They're mine, all mine. They'll get special treatment when I go into action. I treat them with the same consideration and kindness that parents give the child who honors them" (Mal. 3:16–17 MSG).

Wow! Isn't this gracious of our God and King? Who indeed is like Him, merciful, kind, and generous, whose compassions fail not and are new every morning? Great is the Lord and greatly to be praised! Let the picture you paint of God be a beautiful one, one that causes others to want to know Him and have a relationship with Him. A praise report about God's faithfulness encourages and challenges others to put their trust in Him. So give one always! You know God is not complicated in His ways or dealings with man, nor does He want our lives to be complicated. This is why Jesus came, so that we can have the abundant life God designed for us and so that we can show forth God's praise (see Isaiah 43:21).

It is my prayer that your words will always be encouraging to one another and will always declare God's faithfulness. Never be tired of praising His name. His victories on our behalf are always glorious and worth talking about, don't you think? Declare His wonderful works; let the whole world know that Jesus saves and that He is alive forever more! Sing it out! Jehovah is His name! The One who is mighty to save! He loves to hear your voice, so sing out.

A Reason to Sing—Deborah's Song

"Listen, O you kings and princes, For I shall sing about the Lord, The God of Israel" (Judg. 5:3 LB).

Judges 5:1 begins with these words: "Then sang Deborah and Barak" (KJV). Now, what could they possibly be singing about? You see, Israel had just experienced a wonderful victory over Jabin, king of Hazor's army. The entire army was completely destroyed; not one man was left alive to tell a story except Sisera, the commander in chief of the army. He managed to escape to the tent of a woman called Jael, the wife of Heber the Kenite, thinking he would be safe there because of the "mutual-assistance agreement between King Jabin of Hazor and the clan of Heber"(Judg. 4:17 LB). But he was wrong! The very place he ran to for safety was the place where he was killed by none other than the woman he thought would protect him from those pursuing him.

The prophetess Deborah, the wife of Lappidoth and Israel's leader at that time, along with Barak and all Israel, who had just witnessed this huge defeat of their enemies at the hand of God (see Judg. 4:15–16), could not help but rejoice in God's goodness to them. Then they sang about the great victory. You will have to pardon me for saying this, and if you disagree with me, I can understand, but I truly believe Deborah did most of the singing and talking about God's faithfulness. She was the lead worship singer. If you look closely at some of the verses in Judges 5, you will notice some profound prophetic utterances. Being a prophetess of the Most High God, it came naturally to her to declare the Word of the Lord. There were outbursts of "Praise the Lord!" Sounds to me like Deborah the prophetess was doing two things here: not only was she giving thanks to the Lord herself, but she s also was giving a command to the others to praise the Lord (Judg. 5:10). What was she saying by this command? That everyone should sing to the Lord! Deborah was being an example to the people she was called to lead. See her words in Judg. 5:3: "For I shall sing about the Lord, the God of Israel." I paraphrase this as "This is what I am going to do—sing about the Lord God of Israel—and no one can stop me." Deborah, in my book, was letting everyone know this was her thing—to praise the Lord—something she was not just talking about but going to do and was doing, even at that moment.

Next, Deborah is seen declaring the power and greatness of God. "The earth trembled and the sky poured down its rain. Yes, even Mount Sinai quaked at the presence of the God of Israel … the very stars of heaven fought Sisera. The rushing Kishon River swept them away" (Judg. 5:4–5, 20). What a beautiful picture of the power and greatness of God at work! In Judges 5:12 we see Deborah reminding herself to be alert (not to grow weary) but to keep on singing of the mercies of the Lord. She also encourages Barak to arise as well. You know, sometimes we need to remind ourselves and others to sing (to talk about the mercies and goodness of the Lord God), to remember His goodness and the things He has done for us—how He has protected us from evil and how He loves us so. This is something I do all the time. I constantly remind myself and my children to remember God's goodness to us and never to take His mercies for granted. Paul said in Galatians 2:21, "I am not one of those who treats Christ's death as meaningless" (LB). This is how we should live daily—not treat God's mercies and kindness as meaningless. You would feel hurt and disappointed if someone you loved treated a very expensive gift you gave him or her as meaningless, wouldn't you?

We are also told in this chapter that the village musicians sang over and over again of the triumphs of the Lord and that God had saved Israel. Do you inspire people around you to sing or talk about the goodness of the Lord? Live a life of thanksgiving so that others can follow your example. This is why God gives us testimonies (praise reports) all the time, so that others can draw strength and courage to believe Him for their own miracles and live for Him as well. "Yes, bless the Lord!" they sang (Judg. 5:2 LB). In other words, go on; don't stop doing what you are doing and that is blessing the Lord. Truly it is good to give thanks to the Lord! God is magnified when we praise Him. I cannot emphasize this enough. You ought to try blessing the Lord. You will love it!

The woman described in Proverbs 31:26 is a woman whose words are wise. Esther, who became queen after Vashti was forever banished from King Ahasuerus's presence, spoke a totally different language. In her case, she was not "singing to the Lord," but with her words she could be seen surrendering her will to God's purposes. "Though it is strictly forbidden, I will go in to see the king; *and if I perish, I perish*" (Est. 4:16 LB, emphasis added). Pretty strong words, don't you think? Yes, but you see, when a person loves the Lord, his or her language changes to reflect where his or her treasure is. When the individual realizes that everything is not about himself or herself but for the glory of God, that person will willingly give up all that matters and will become like the apostle Paul, literally sounding like him and talking like him (see Galatians 2:20). No wonder David, the sweet psalmist of Israel, said, "Let the words of my mouth and the meditation of my heart be acceptable in your sight, O Lord, my [firm, impenetrable] Rock and my Redeemer" (Ps. 19:14 AB).

Later in Esther's story, we see her speaking words of wisdom to God's glory in situations that could have turned very ugly for her and her people, the Jews, right before her eyes. But what did she do? She opened her mouth with wisdom at all times, only letting her language reflect love and respect for the king and for his authority. As I have tried to point out, it is not all about singing (as in singing just any song with a beautiful, melodious voice); it is about having a reason to talk to others about the Lord, His goodness, and His merciful kindness and to show your love and respect to the One who created all things— God, the eternal Creator! Many people would rather not sing and not talk about the Lord, either because they are shy or because they don't want to. But they would rather talk about their pain and sorrow with passion. It's amazing! Let us learn to exercise ourselves in this form of godliness, sharing the love of our Christ and King by speaking about Him and His mercies. "For bodily exercise profits a little, but godliness is profitable for all things, having promise of the life that now is and of that which is to come" (1 Tim. 4:7 8).

You have dozens of reasons to sing, and one of them—the most important—is that you are alive today. Just think! There are thousands of people who were born on the same day you were born who are not alive today. Is it because you are better than they were? You are alive today because God Himself chose to show you His mercy and forgiveness. So let's go out there and sing with all that is within us, and praise His holy name! Let your language, as it becomes the gospel of Christ, be full of faith and thanksgiving and celebrating Jesus!

Chapter 7

Embracing God

Urge me not to leave you or to turn back from following you.
—Ruth 1:16 (AB)

But as for me and my house, we will serve the Lord.
—Joshua 24:15 (AB)

Throughout the Bible, we see men and women holding onto God, His Word, His promises, and everything about Him, including His plans for their lives. Many have walked this walk. God showed up in their lives suddenly and began to work in them and through them in very unusual ways that brought about a transformation in their lives, causing them to surrender their all and to fear Him and love and cherish Him dearly, with all their hearts and all that is within them. His grace was made available to each one during the process of transformation, and that same grace is available to you and me today. You know, it is one thing to say that you are born again and that you love Jesus, but it is an entirely different thing to really, really live your life for the Lord as it becomes the gospel of Christ.

God first loved us and has given us the grace to respond to His love, to embrace Him, and to walk closely with Him (1 John 4:19). But how we walk in this grace depends on each individual entirely. In Psalm 34:1, it is written, "I will bless the Lord at all times; His praise shall continually be in my mouth" (AB). Note the first three words in this verse of Scripture: "I will bless." Here we see that the psalmist was saying clearly that this was something he was going to do himself, something he was determined to do, and that was to bless the Lord. This was not just going to be a one-time thing for him. No sir! It was going to be a continuous thing for him; it was going to be a way of living for him.

How many times have we determined to do something or desired to do something but have not been able to achieve or accomplish that thing, simply because we either allowed the spirit of laziness to come into our lives or because our "self" got in the way, thereby blinding our vision? Please know that when self gets in the way, we lose focus of God's purpose for our lives. And God wants us focused on His purposes for our lives, not distracted! For God is "not willing that any should perish" (2 Peter 3:9 KJV). If anything, He wants us living happy and healthy lifestyles. No wonder Jesus answered the woman at the well, whom He had asked to give Him a drink in John 4:10, in this manner: "If you had only known and had recognized God's gift" (AB).

Unfortunately, there are many out there who do not even recognize the blessings and prosperity that is before them. I believe very strongly that the more we bless the Lord, blessing Him with all that is within us, the easier it becomes to embrace Him, walk with Him, love Him, and abide in Him. In short, we become totally one with God. After all, this was Jesus's prayer to the Father and desire for us in John 17:21. Hear

Him! "My prayer for all of them is … Father—that just as you are in me and I am in you, so they will be in us" (LB).

I encourage you today to clasp the hands of your Creator, God Almighty, and walk with Him into the bright future He has already destined for you. The woman whose life has been transformed by the power of the Most High God knows how to clasp the hands of her Creator without letting go. She knows she can trust Him because she has seen Him work marvelously in her life. God's Word clearly commands us to individually "work out (cultivate, carry out to the goal, and fully complete) your own salvation with reverence and awe and trembling (self-distrust, with serious caution, tenderness of conscience, watchfulness against temptation, timidly shrinking from whatever might offend God and discredit the name of Christ)" (Phil. 2:12 AB).

Here are a few principle steps you can take to daily exercise yourself so that you can fully embrace God for who He is. These principles are seen all through the Scriptures. I assure you there are many other ways you can walk out this spiritual exercise of embracing God, but I will only mention ten basic ones I personally consider important. So here we go!

Step One: Decide

> "But as for me, I will sing each morning about
> your power and mercy" (Ps. 59:16 LB).

You have to decide for yourself (no one else can make that decision for you) that you are going to embrace God—for you and not for another—for who He is: love (and not for who the unbelieving in heart have portrayed Him to be, especially in their minds). You have to make up your mind that this is what you are going to do and how you are going to live each day—embrace Him, embrace His love, commune with Him in prayer, and speak of Him to all who care to hear you sing of His mercies each new day. Your decision is very important, and if you are undecided, wavering back and forth, unsure of what you want, you will not find stability in your life. "[For being as he is] a man of two minds (hesitating, dubious, irresolute), [he is] unstable and unreliable and uncertain about everything [he thinks, feels decides]" (James 1:8 AB). In Psalm 103:1, we are instructed to bless the Lord with all that is within us. I love what it says in the Amplified Bible:

"Bless (affectionately, gratefully praise) the Lord … and all that is [deepest] within me, bless His holy name!" You know, the woman who had been sick for twelve years with internal bleeding, in Matthew 9, decided for herself that she was going to make every effort to try to touch the hem of Jesus's garment for her healing. She believed if she did this she would be healed. She decided for herself to embrace the power of God that was available to her for her healing and deliverance right there and then, not wavering in her faith. Every time you and I decide (note the key word here is *decide*) to step out in faith to embrace God, miracles happen. God's power is released to transform, deliver, heal, restore, and forgive for whatever situation. The Samaritan woman at the well, in John 4, decided she was going to embrace Jesus and the words He had spoken to her, and she did not stop there. She also decided to tell others about Him.

Will you take a step of faith today to live each day in blessing the name of the Lord? I tell you it will be good for your soul.

Step Two: Worship God Earnestly

"They began to worship [God] in earnest" (Hag. 1:12 LB).

The key word here is *earnestly*. How earnest are you in your dealings toward God and with man? Don't be like those who say things they do not mean. Be honest and sincere in whatever it is that you do before God and before men. Why did these people decide to earnestly worship God? Here is the highlight from Haggai 1, without telling the whole story. God had just sent His Word through His servant, the prophet Haggai, to His people to reveal His will for them and also to warn them. And because of the severity of the warning from the Lord, Zerubbabel, the governor at that time, along with Joshua, the high priest, with all the remnants of the people who had returned from captivity, chose to obey Haggai's message from the Lord "not vaguely or partly, but completely" (Hag. 1:12 AB). The result: they immediately began to worship God in earnest, giving Him the reverence, the respect, and the worthiness that was His due. Worship is not just about singing a slow song of praise. It is about giving God all the glory, all the honor, all the respect, and the reverence that is His due, which He rightly deserves as God Almighty. God is a God to be feared! Hence, the warning in Galatians 6:7,

> "Do not be deceived and deluded and misled; God will not allow Himself to be sneered at (scorned, disdained, or mocked by mere pretensions, or professions, or by His precepts being set aside). [He inevitably deludes himself who attempts to delude God.] For whatever a man sows, that and that only is what he will reap" (AB).

So you see, this is what the fear of the Lord will do to you: it will cause you to *earnestly* give honor, worship, and reverence to God. A person used to having his or her own way and doing his or her own thing can only go so far. Remember the story of the prodigal son who wandered away to a far country, and squandered all the wealth he inherited from his father, and ended up in abject poverty? (Luke

15:11–32). God always has the final say! His mercies endure forever (Ps.136)! Because He loves us so much, God will always do everything to bring us back to Him. He is love!

So let us fear the Lord and depart from evil (Prov. 3:7). Let us embrace Him with everything we've got, earnestly, in spirit and in truth. Don't wait for someone to tell you to worship God earnestly before you do, and don't wait for a situation to arise before you worship Him. He is God and worthy of your worship of Him.

Step Three: Long for Fellowship with Him

> "As the hart pants and longs for the water brooks, so
> I pant and long for you, O God. My inner self thirsts
> for God, for the living God. When shall I come
> and behold the face of God?" (Ps. 42:1–2 AB).

Jesus said, "If any man is thirsty, let Him come to Me and drink!" (John 7:37 AB). Long for His presence! Long for Him! A desire to be in His presence continually should be the longing of your soul and the cry of your heart. Read the words of the psalmist.

> O God, my God! How I search for you! How I thirst for you
> in this parched and weary land where there is no water.
> How I long to find you! How I wish I could go into your
> sanctuary to see your strength and glory, for your love
> and kindness are better to me than life itself. How I praise
> you! I will bless you as long as I live, lifting up my hands
> to you in prayer … I will praise you with great joy. I will
> lie awake at night thinking of you … I follow close behind
> you. (Ps. 63:1–8 LB)

What a heart cry! What a longing of the soul! Did you notice how many times he said these words: "How I"? Only God can satisfy the longing of your soul. In this passage of Scripture, the psalmist, after calling on the name of the Lord, said these very powerful words: "How I search for you!" You know something? If you do not earnestly seek or search for something (e.g., your car keys, precious jewelry), you might not find what you are looking for. And this brings us to the next step, which is the principle of seeking God.

Step Four: Seek the Lord with All Your Heart

"Seek, inquire for, and require the Lord while He may
be found [claiming Him by necessity and by right];
call upon Him while He is near" (Isa. 55:6 AB).

To seek means to search for. And when you seek for God with all of your heart, you will find Him because God Himself said so. And God cannot lie (Num. 3:19). In the book of Jeremiah, God says, "Then you will seek Me, inquire for, and require Me [as a vital necessity] and find Me when you search for Me with all your heart" (29:13 AB).

Seeking for someone or something requires effort. Time is required when seeking the Lord; patience is required; a desperation and not hesitation is involved and required; energy is required; and hope is required—the hope that you will find what you are looking for. Jesus gives a beautiful illustration of what seeking entails in Luke 15:8. "Or what woman, having ten silver coins, if she loses one coin, does not light a lamp, sweep the house, and search carefully until she finds it?" (NKJV). If you seek the Lord with all of your heart, you will find Him, because the Word of God tells us to seek. Matthew 7:7–8 says, "Seek, and you will find … and he who seeks finds"(NKJV). I pray you may seek the Lord with all your heart, not just today, not just in your hour of need but every moment of every day of your life.

Step Five: Wait on the Lord

"But those who wait for the Lord [who expect, look for, and hope in Him] shall change and renew their strength and power; they shall lift their wings and mount up [close to God] as eagles [mount up to the sun]; they shall run and not be weary, they shall walk and not faint or become tired" (Isa. 40:31 AB).

"I waited patiently for God to help me; then He listened and heard my cry. He lifted me out of the pit of despair, out from the bog and mire, and set my feet on a hard, firm path, and steadied me as I walked along" (Ps. 40:1–2 LB).

Waiting involves remaining inactive in readiness or expectation. You cannot embrace God without having to wait (taking time away from your usual busy, busy schedule) in silent praise ("O God in Zion, we wait before you in silent praise, and thus fulfill our vow" [Ps. 65:1 LB]). We wait because those who wait on God renew their strength and also because the Lord answers prayers ("And because you answer prayer, all mankind will come to you with their requests" [Ps. 65:2 LB]). When you choose to wait on the Lord, you will definitely experience a renewing of strength. Weariness gives way to the strength of the Lord that comes upon you in that time of silent praise to refresh, renew, and energize you, both spiritually and physically. Acts 1:4 tells us to "wait for the Promise of the Father" (NKJV), for there is the fulfillment of the promises of God in waiting. "For we through the Spirit eagerly wait for the hope of righteousness by faith" (Gal. 5:5 NKJV).

Step Six: Trust

> "If you want favor with both God and man, and a reputation
> for good judgment and common sense, then trust the Lord
> completely; don't ever trust yourself" (Prov. 3:4–5 LB).

The issue of trust is very important, especially in any relationship. "I believe you! I believe your Word is true! My confidence is in you! I know you love me and care for my well-being! You are the hope that I have!"

Years ago, while vacationing in London, I was walking and just praying for my children, who were much younger at that time. I suddenly heard the voice of the Spirit of the Lord say to me, "You do not trust me to take care of your children." To say the least, I was shocked by those words because I did not think that was the case. But as I allowed myself to think on the words spoken to me and allowed them to sink in, I had to honestly admit to myself—and to the Lord— that I was guilty. I realized, there and then, that I had unconsciously allowed fear to rule my heart where my children were concerned. This I expressed by way of hardly letting them out of my sight. I did not realize it then, but now I see that I was not being an overly protective mother but a mother whose actions and decisions concerning her children were ruled by fear. Fear is a spirit, and it involves torment (1 John 4:18); in other words, it is crippling.

Bottom line: I was totally under the influence of the spirit of fear and never fully realized that I was its slave and was bound by it. And this fear spilled over to the children, while presenting itself to me as my being a protective mom. Here I was, a praying mother who said she trusted God, who daily prayed to Him yet would not let Him have His way in the lives of the children He'd given to me.

With tears in my eyes, I truly repented and asked for forgiveness on that street in London. You know, it is one thing to pray to God about something, and it is totally different to step out of the way, and let Him have His way. This is where the issue of trust comes in. Isn't it strange how people will go to other people for help because they trust them? They go to attorneys to help them write their wills, and they trust them to execute their wills after their deaths. Children trust their parents to take care of them. When a man and a woman come together to get married, it is because they love and trust one another. So why is it so hard for us humans to trust in the living God? I believe fear has something to do with it.

The Word of God encourages us to trust in the Lord because whoever does is "happy, blessed, and fortunate" (Prov. 16:20 AB). Sad to say, even today people are still looking for people, places, or things in which to put their trust and confidence. Psalm 20:7 says, "Some trust in chariots, and some in horses." Today, there are still some people who trust in their wealth and not in the living God. When you trust in God, He will show you His salvation and make your way glorious. Psalm 32:10 beautifully highlights this: "But he who trusts in the Lord, mercy shall surround him" (NKJV).

Step Seven: Willingness

> "If you are willing and obedient you shall eat
> the good of the land" (Isa. 1:19 AB).

You have to be *willing* (i.e., to be without reluctance) to embrace God at all times. Of the Corinthian Church, Paul had this to say: "For I bear witness that according to their ability, yes, and beyond their ability, they were freely willing ... And not only as we had hoped, but they first gave themselves to the Lord" (2 Cor. 8:3, 5 NKJV). Willingness is a form of sacrifice—it is the sacrifice of the giving of oneself to be a blessing to another. Its expression of giving and service without reluctance or reservation is a reflection of the heart of a man or woman. Now, this is not to say that there aren't those who willingly give themselves to commit evil works. On the contrary, there are a lot of people out there who willingly live a lifestyle of evil.

Every day on the radio, in the newspapers, and on the television, we hear stories of people being murdered or raped. Even in the days of Paul the apostle, there were those who willingly gave themselves over to do evil—to kill Paul (Acts 23:12–15).

I encourage you to willingly embrace God's outstretched loving arms that reach out to you, so that you can enjoy the blessings He has in store for you. "Whosoever will, let him take the water of life freely" (Rev. 22:17 KJV). Be a willing giver today!

Step Eight: Pray

"Men always ought to pray and not lose heart" (Luke 18:1 NKJV).

"Pray without ceasing" (1 Thess. 5:17 NKJV).

"You will make your prayer to Him, and He
will hear you" (Job 22:27 AB).

Praying is another principle I consider important. Through prayers, you are able to embrace God firmly. Prayer is like an anchor, firmly holding your faith in place; that is, in trusting the living God. It is your heart connection to God, your means of communicating with Him. It is just like breathing. When a person stops breathing completely, he or she is pronounced dead. Just as a person needs air to breath, so a person needs to have a prayer lifestyle so that he or she lives in the fullness of God's blessing while alive. Prayer is the key that unlocks doors. But to have those doors unlocked, you have to embrace God at all times—in and through prayers. Jesus taught us in Matthew 6:9–13 to pray along these lines:

> "Our Father in heaven, we honor your holy name. We ask that your kingdom will come now. May your will be done here on earth, just as it is in heaven. Give us our food again today, as usual, and forgive us our sins, just as we have forgiven those who have sinned against us. Don't bring us into temptation, but deliver us from the evil one. Amen" (LB).

Why does Jesus encourage praying in this manner? Because He knows that through prayers we learn to commune with God, seeing Him as God, and then come to recognize Him as our Father, as one to honor, as one whose will shall be done on earth as it is in heaven, and as the one who provides for our needs, forgives sins, and delivers from the Evil One. To have your needs met, you have to learn to open your mouth and call on the name of the Lord in prayer. God is waiting for you! Just call on Him!

In Jeremiah 33:3, God says, "Call to Me and I will answer you, and show you great and mighty things which you do not know" (NKJV). So here is your free pass from God. Why not use it right now? Go ahead! Call on Him (pray), and He will answer you and show you what you need to know or do.

Step Nine: Praise and Thanksgiving

> "Therefore by Him let us continually offer the sacrifice
> of praise to God, that is the fruit of our lips, giving
> thanks to His name" (Heb. 13:15 NKJV).

> "In everything give thanks; for this is the will of God
> in Christ Jesus for you" (1 Thess. 5:18 NKJV).

The key words here are *continually* and *offer*. If we choose to live the lifestyle of offering praise and thanksgiving to God, our Father and King, then we should do so continually, day after day, night after night, without ceasing, for God is worthy of all praise. Psalm 33:1 tells us that "praise is becoming and appropriate for those who are upright [in heart]" (AB). The next verse encourages us to "give thanks to the Lord" and to "sing praises to Him." I encourage you today to make praising God a lifestyle. You will definitely be the better for it—I can tell you from experience. Praising God causes the atmosphere around you to become saturated with His awesome, glorious presence, which brings deliverance for you and gives you great victories all around. And darkness has no choice but to flee, because in His presence there is fullness of joy (Ps. 16:11), He is the Light that shines in darkness, and darkness does not comprehend this Light (John 1:5). Jesus says of Himself, "I am the light of the world. He who follows Me shall not walk in darkness, but have the light of life" (John 8:12 NKJV).

Step Ten: Hope

> "Now hope does not disappoint, because the love of
> God has been poured out in our hearts by the Holy
> Spirit who was given to us" (Rom. 5:5 NKJV).

> "Hope in God" (Ps. 42:11 NKJV).

"Hope in God," the psalmist said. Now, why would he say something like that? Because from experience, he had come to know the faithfulness of God—that God never fails, and hope in Him never disappoints. For God loves each of us dearly. So my question to you now is this: in what or in whom have you put your hope? The Bible encourages you to hope in God because He is the help of your countenance and your God (Ps. 43:5). And in Him only can you find everlasting joy.

We are told in Job 8:13 that "the hope of the hypocrite [the "godless," according to the Amplified Bible] shall perish" (NKJV). But those who wait on the Lord, who hope and trust in His mercy, will never be ashamed (Ps. 25:3). Do you want all of your hopes dashed? I don't think so! So why not hope in God? For you will yet praise Him who is the help of your countenance.

The Living Bible translation of Psalm 42:11 says, "Expect God to act!" Wow! Do you expect God to act on your behalf all the time? If you do not embrace Him fully, if you don't hold on to Him, don't trust Him, and don't have faith in Him at all, how then can you expect Him to act on your behalf? Hebrews 11:6 says, "For he who comes to God must believe that He is, and that He is a rewarder of those who diligently seek him" (NKJV). Like the psalmist said to himself in Psalm 42:11, so I say to you too and encourage you to tell yourself, not just today but daily: don't give up or be upset but hope in God, for the time will come, and you will definitely and joyfully praise Him, the help of your countenance.

These are just a few principles in which you can walk to exercise yourself in godliness. God does not come to take from us. He wants to add to us, to bless us, and to prosper us, and He needs us to take that step of faith in coming to Him. This is why Jesus said to us, "Come to Me, all you who labor and are heavy laden, and I will give you rest. Take My yoke upon you and learn from Me, for I am gentle and lowly in heart, and you will find rest for your souls. For My yoke is easy and My burden is light" (Matt. 11:28–30 NKJV).

I encourage you: do not be like those who say to God, "Depart from us, for we do not desire the knowledge of Your ways. Who is the Almighty that we should serve Him? And what profit do we have if we should pray to Him?" (Job 21:14–15 NKJV). Hear the Word of the Lord! In the very next verse, it is written, "Indeed their prosperity is not in their hand." So please embrace God with all that is within you, because your success in life, your prosperity in life, and your ability to do things is not in your hands but in the hands of the almighty God, the Creator of all things. Let go of yourself, embrace God, and get to live the abundant life He wants for you.

Conclusion

Jesus said, "Man shall not live by bread alone, but by every word that proceeds from the mouth of God" (Matt. 4:4). God knows that by His Word we are warned, reminded, enlightened, and instructed on how to live for Him in this world. "Moreover, by them is Your servant warned (reminded, illuminated, and instructed); and in keeping them there is great reward" (Ps. 19:11 AB).

Paul said, "For to me, living means opportunities for Christ" (Phil. 1:21 LB). God wants us to live, and He clearly states this in His Word: "And when I passed by you and saw you rolling about in your blood, I said to you in your blood, *Live!* Yes, I said to you still in your natal blood, *Live!*" (Ezek. 16:6 AB, emphasis added). If Jesus had not died on the cross for us, we would not be privileged to enjoy the eternal life God has given us—the grace and ability to live in Him and to live for Him, His purpose, and His glory.

For us to continue to live in Him and for Him, we need to renew our minds daily with God's precious Word, which transforms us on the inside (Rom. 12:2). While transformation is an ongoing process (God working in us to give us a hope and a bright future), we need to remember that we ourselves still have our own parts to play to be able to remain alive in Him until Christ is formed in us.

"Work out (cultivate, carry out to the goal, and fully complete) your own salvation with reverence and awe and trembling (self-distrust, with serious caution, tenderness of conscience, watchfulness against temptation, timidly shrinking from whatever might offend God and discredit the name of Christ)" (Phil. 2:12 AB).

Today, I encourage you, just as His Word says,

> Now acquaint yourself with Him, and be at peace; thereby good will come to you. Receive, please, instruction from His mouth, and lay up His words in your heart. If you return to the Almighty, you will be built up; You will remove iniquity far from your tents. Then you will lay your gold in the dust … Yes, the Almighty will be your gold and your precious silver; for then you will have your delight in the Almighty, and lift up your face to God. You will make your prayer to Him, He will hear you … and it will be established for you; so light will shine on your ways. When they cast you down, and you say, "Exaltation will come!" (Job 22:21–29 NKJV)

How about that? How wonderfully easy God has made it for you and me to live in His love and mercy! Accept God's love now, and let Him be your light and your salvation. You can never receive God's favor or this new way of living by trying to do things on your own or in your own way. God's Word says that by ourselves we can do nothing. But in Christ we can do all things (John 15:5; Phil. 4:13). Just open your mouth, and God will fill it (Ps. 81:10). Know this: "It's in Christ that we find out who we are and what we are living for" (Eph. 1:11 MSG). Only in Christ Jesus and none other!

Printed in the United States
By Bookmasters